T5-CVN-553

The Writing and Reading Process
A New Approach to Literacy

Resource Guide

James Whitney
Ruth Hubbard

With Rick Littlefield

Developed from events recorded during a
two-year research study conducted by
Jane Hansen and Donald Graves.

Heinemann
Portsmouth, NH

ISBN 0-435-08433-X

Heinemann Educational Books, Inc.
70 Court Street   Portsmouth, NH   03801

London • Edinburgh • Melbourne • Auckland
Hong Kong • Singapore • Kuala Lumpur
New Delhi • Ibadan • Nairobi • Johannesburg
Kingston • Port of Spain

This Resource Guide has been designed to be easy to use in a workshop setting. The loose-leaf format allows you to insert the sections in the order you wish, and you can insert materials of your own, where appropriate, for the individual needs of your workshop and the participants.

ISBN 0-435-08433-X (Resource Guide)

Printed and manufactured in the United States of America.

10 9 8 7 6 5 4 3 2 1

Contents

A Note on the Videotapes and the Resource Guide

These videotapes document "real-world" events—nothing has been contrived or added to enhance the process for television. The same care and attention has been used in editing to preserve the authenticity of the moment.

This Resource Guide provides tips on viewing and setting up workshops around each of the three videos in the program *The Writing and Reading Process: A New Approach to Literacy*. The first section of this guide, "Using Television and Videotape Effectively," explains how to make the most of the video medium. Following that are sections for each of the three videos in the program: "Time and Choice: Key Elements for Process Teaching"; "One Classroom: A Child's View"; and "Writing Conference Principles: The Child Learns, The Teacher Learns." The three videos in this program can be used either separately or together, and in any sequence.

The sections of this Resource Guide relating to the videotapes are all organized similarly. We have provided a data sheet for each tape, which gives an overview of the tape's contents and an indication of where on the tape the different topics can be found. Following the data sheet are notes on how the tape can be used in a workshop setting, along with articles and other handouts that supplement the tape. Finally, at the end of each tape Resource Guide section is a bibliography of books and articles related to the subject of the tape.

The overall purpose of this Resource Guide is to help you make the best use of the tapes in a workshop setting. The loose-leaf format allows you to insert the sections in the order you wish, and you can insert materials of your own, where appropriate, for the particular needs of your workshop and the participants.

Using Television and Videotape Effectively

Understanding the Medium

Television brings us close to events that we could experience in no other way. Whether the scene is a breathtaking view from the top of Mt. Everest, a tour through the intricate workings of the human heart, or the classroom scenes from these tapes, televised sights and sounds come to us with realism beyond anything civilization has experienced before.

Watching a program from start to finish is a little like watching a parade—it passes in review, and then it is gone. Most of the time—when the objectives are to entertain and inform—this is enough. But, when the objective is to learn, a static vantage point does not allow us freedom to study. Suddenly, information comes too fast, with no flexibility to alter the pace and no opportunity to look again. As we attempt to process information at a rate beyond our capacity, frustration and boredom are likely to overtake us.

STOPPING TIME

When events are recorded on videotape, they become captured. The VCR enables us to stop the parade of information at any point, freeze it in time, and review it for a more detailed look. When our objective is to learn, controlling the flow of information in this way is essential.

MANAGING INFORMATION

Books—mainstays of learning throughout the centuries—are valuable tools because they empower us to control our learning experience. The VCR allows us to do the same thing with visual materials. Books and VCRs allow us to *refer to an index*, *scan* rapidly through text, and pull out only what we need. We can *start* and *stop*—wherever and whenever we wish. We can review difficult concepts slowly and precisely, until we understand. And a simple system of numbers leads us back to important information—instantly.

Figure 1 provides a closer look at the controls that allow us to manipulate time and information through a VCR.

VCR FUNCTIONS

Here are some functions commonly available on VCRs.

Start/Stop
The "Start" and "Stop" controls simply enable you to start the VCR when you are ready to watch and stop when you've seen enough!

Pause
The "Pause" button puts everything on hold. You can use the "Pause" function to stop and reflect, take notes, or freeze an image on the screen for closer scrutiny.

Some machines hold this "still-life" image better than others. Old or inexpensive VCRs may have only two video heads—and their ability to freeze an image clearly is very poor. Newer or more expensive machines with four or more video heads can freeze the image with negligible loss of picture quality.

FIGURE 1 VCR Front Panel, Showing Control Buttons

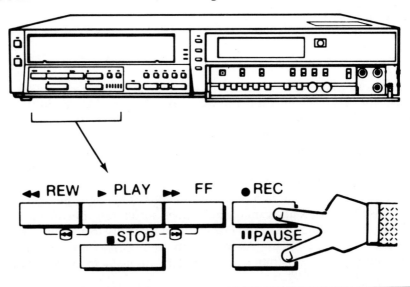

To avoid damaging the tape, all machines automatically switch from "Pause" to "Stop" after approximately seven minutes.

High-Speed Search (Scan)

Most VCRs can play pictures back at several times the normal viewing speed—in both forward and reverse directions. This feature enables you to search through tapes quickly to find specific segments. Once again, some machines do this better than others. VCRs with the two-head system severely distort the high-speed image with large horizontal bands of visual noise (snow). (See Figure 2.) This makes high-speed viewing very difficult. Machines with four or more heads produce clear high-speed images (Figure 3). These images cause much less eyestrain and mental fatigue—something to consider if you plan to use the scanning feature a lot.

Counters

All VCRs come with built-in counters. (See Figure 4.) Counters help you locate recorded information quickly and consistently. To *index* important events for future reference, make a *tape log*, or *data sheet* (samples of which are provided for each tape in this series—see the chapters of this Viewing Guide for the tape segments).

Here's how to do it:

1. Rewind the tape to the beginning and set the counter at zero.
2. Play the tape through, pausing the tape to write down counter numbers at the key points you wish to recall.

Store the log with your tape for future reference. A word of caution, however: VCR counters do *not* speak a universal language—they all count

FIGURE 2   High-Speed Image with a Two-Head VCR

FIGURE 3   High-Speed Image with a Four-Head VCR

FIGURE 4 Counter on Front of VCR

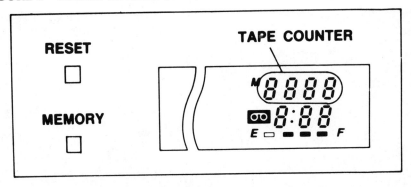

differently. If you are using a different machine, you may need to prepare a new log.

Auto-Search
Many institutional VCRs offer optional "Auto-Search" counters. (See Figure 5.) These enable you to access any portion of your tape automatically by dialing the appropriate counter numbers on a keypad.

FIGURE 5 Auto-Search Controller

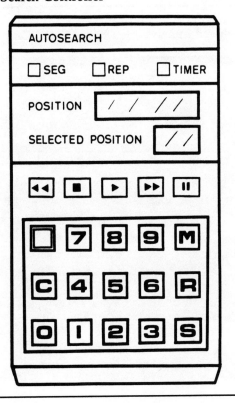

Most auto-search devices feature built-in memories, which function as electronic bookmarks. The memory function allows you to index your tape with up to sixty "begin" and "end" times. As you enter each one, the auto-search controller stores it. When you are finished, the completed index is automatically "written" on the beginning of the tape for future use.

Learning to use all of your VCR's features will increase the machine's value to you as a teaching tool. Familiarity has another benefit, too. If you know your machine well, you will feel more confident operating it in front of a group.

Putting on a Presentation

Staging a video presentation is easy—if you know what you need and you know what to do. Here is a guide to help you make the presentation both effective and successful.

WHAT MAKES A GOOD VIEWING AREA?

An Echo-Free Room

Many classrooms are rectangular with untreated walls, ceilings, and floors. Sound from the television speaker bounces off these parallel surfaces, making it difficult to hear clearly. Look for spaces with irregular shapes, carpets, drapes, room dividers—anything that will absorb sound and diminish echo. The area should also be well removed from noisy activities and equipment.

Light Control

Look for areas where the lights can be dimmed—or completely shut off—in the front of the room. Some light is necessary for taking notes and preventing eyestrain. But too much will cause glare on the screen and make viewing difficult.

Seating

Each viewer needs a desk, table, hard-cover folder, or some other kind of writing surface. If furniture is movable, make a semicircle around the television to facilitate viewing and discussion. Tiered seating, as in a movie theater, is ideal.

Height of Screen

The television screen should be high enough to permit viewing without obstruction, but not too high for people in the front rows. A table or audiovisual cart between 42 and 54 inches in height will tilt the television slightly forward to favor front-row viewing. If a standard 29-inch table is all you have, consider placing a chair or some other suitable object on top of it to raise the viewing height.

WHAT EQUIPMENT DO I NEED?

The Screen

The picture must be large enough so that everyone can see it properly. A popular rule of thumb is *one inch of screen per person*. Under most conditions, a class of twenty students can easily view programming on a 21-inch television set. However, if your room is very wide or irregular in shape, an additional set may be required to give everyone a clear view. The necessary cable and signal splitter for adding a second set can be purchased at most hardware or video stores. Check with your AV department—the school district may own the necessary equipment or have a rental agreement with a local video store.

Sound

The sound on many televisions becomes distorted when the volume is turned up to fill the classroom. Distorted sound quickly leads to fatigue and inat-

Using Television and Videotape Effectively

tention. If you are unable to get enough clean sound from your viewing set-up, plug a small hi-fi amplifier or PA system into the "Audio Output" jack of the VCR. Your audience will be more content as a result.

Scheduling Equipment

WHERE DO I GO FOR EQUIPMENT AND HELP?

Be sure to schedule televisions, carts, and other equipment with your school media specialist, librarian, or designated caretaker well in advance—most schools loan equipment on a first-come, first-served basis. If you are also reserving a VCR, give both *the cassette format* (VHS, Beta, or U-Matic) and *the recording speed* (Beta 1 or VHS SP). Pick the equipment up ahead of time so you can become familiar with the machine's controls and indexing counter.

Finding Help

Learning how to set up and use equipment can be an intimidating assignment. However, help is almost always available. If your school has a media specialist, seek that person out for advice and assistance. Also, check with your school librarian or resource center aide. Many of these people have special media training. Finally, look for your school's "electronic wizards"—teachers or students who know a lot about VCRs, big-screen video, and sound reinforcement. Any of these people could help you plan the room layout and set up the equipment.

Allow plenty of time to iron out problems. Last-minute surprises are no fun—especially when you have a room full of people staring at you!

SETTING UP FOR THE PRESENTATION

Arrange the Room

1. If possible, arrange chairs in a semicircle around the television. This creates a good environment for viewing and discussion.
2. Draw the curtains or blinds, and check the illumination. Is it light enough to take notes, yet dark enough to see the picture clearly?
3. Are there distracting noises that will interfere with the presentation? If so, can they be turned off or blocked out?
4. Will everyone have access to a writing surface?

Check out the Playback System

Load your cassette into the VCR and run it. Adjust the controls for what you think will be the best settings. Then walk around the room and check the playback from a variety of locations:

1. Is there any distracting glare on the screen?
2. Is the image clear? Are the color and contrast good?
3. Are titles and other printed messages readable from the back of the room?
4. Is the audio loud and clear? It should almost be too loud during the test, since much sound will be absorbed when the room is full of people.

Check Your Indexing

If the VCR you use has a different counter or indexing system from the one you used originally, you have two options: re-catalogue the tape on that VCR; or use the high-speed search function to visually locate starting points.

In Case of Trouble

Most of the problems that occur during video presentations are minor, and easily corrected if you know what to do. Keep this checklist handy when you set up for your presentation.

If you're unable to insert the cassette into the VCR, check the following:

1. Is the machine plugged in and turned on?
2. Is the cassette being inserted correctly? (See Figure 6.)
3. Is there a cassette already in the machine?

CANNOT INSERT THE CASSETTE

If the VCR accepts the cassette, but the function buttons won't work, check to see if the "Dew" or "Moisture" warning light is on. This frequently happens when cold machines or tapes are brought into a warm room and then operated before condensation can evaporate. If this is the problem, *leave the machine on.* An internal heater will purge moisture in 15 to 20 minutes, and the machine will reset itself for normal operation.

VCR ACCEPTS CASSETTE, BUT FUNCTION BUTTONS DO NOT WORK

FIGURE 6   Inserting a Cassette

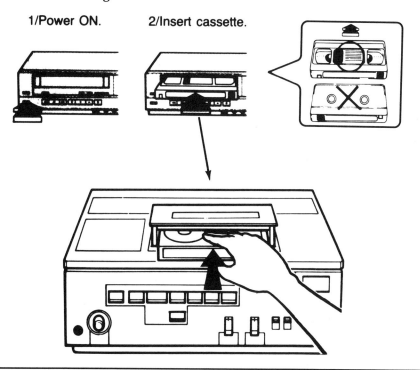

1/Power ON.   2/Insert cassette.

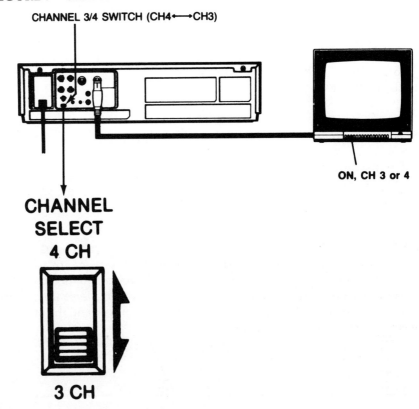

FIGURE 7 Channel Selector Switch

CHANNEL 3/4 SWITCH (CH4◄──►CH3)

ON, CH 3 or 4

CHANNEL
SELECT
4 CH

3 CH

NO PICTURE—OR NOISY (SNOWY) PICTURE—DURING PLAYBACK

If you're having trouble getting a clear picture, or *any* picture, check the following:

1. Most VCRs have a miniature built-in "television transmitter" (called an "RF Unit") that sends the signal to your television set on either channel 3 or channel 4. Somewhere on the VCR there is a small channel selector switch that chooses which channel the VCR will use. (See Figure 7.) If the picture quality is poor, make sure your TV set and VCR are on the same channel. If they are, and the picture is still poor, try adjusting the "fine-tuning" control on the television set.

2. Streaking and breaking up of the picture could be due to a tracking error. Find the VCR's "Tracking Control" (Figure 8) and rotate it slowly in either direction while observing the screen. If the problem is tracking error, the picture will clear.

3. There could be faulty cables. Wiggle, tighten, and substitute them (in that order) until you find the problem.

If these steps fail to correct the problem, refer to the "Troubleshooting" section of your VCR operating manual for more detailed instructions.

FIGURE 8   Tracking Control and How It Affects the Picture

Tracking Control

Time and Choice: Key Elements for Process Teaching

Data Sheet for "Time and Choice: Key Elements for Process Teaching"

Note: Zero counter when Heinemann logo disappears.

Segment No.	Beginning	End	Contents
1	00:18	3:44	Time for writing
2	3:44	6:59	Time for reading
3	7:00	7:31	Choosing writing topics
4	7:31	7:52	Methods to help children choose topics
		STRATEGIES FOR FINDING NEW IDEAS	
5	7:52	8:08	Whole class sessions
6	8:08	8:45	Teacher conferences
7	8:45	9:41	Children conversing with one another
		CHOOSING READING MATERIAL	
8	10:56	12:28	How ideas for book choice are generated
9	12:28	13:09	Children reading books of their choice regularly
10	13:09	14:35	Teachers offering new advice and assistance for book choice—Leslie's system
11	14:35	16:07	Phyllis's approach
12	16:07	16:43	Pat's approach
13	16:43	18:02	Choosing books that the teacher hasn't read
		WRITING/READING AND THE RESOURCE BASE	
14	18:02	18:26	Community and parents
15	18:26	20:15	Within the school
16	20:15	22:04	Writing/reading—enthusiasm both in school and at home

Suggestions for the Use of "Time and Choice: Key Elements for Process Teaching"

How can you use "Time and Choice" to best suit the needs of your audience? Just like any teaching tool, there is no one right way to use it, but several possibilities. Let's take a look at the ways some people use this tape within a workshop setting, one in a full-day workshop and the other in a three-hour workshop.

FULL-DAY WORKSHOP

Barbara is a reading specialist at Moore School, a K–8 elementary and middle school with a staff of 25 teachers. Most of the teachers at the school are teaching writing with an emphasis on process, and have been teaching writing this way for a few years. As they have become more comfortable with the writing-process philosophy, some of the teachers have begun to make changes in their reading programs to be more consistent with their writing programs. For their upcoming in-service day, they have asked Barbara to conduct a workshop to help them explore some changes they might like to attempt during their reading time, and she has decided to include the tape "Time and Choice: Key Elements for Process Teaching" into this workshop.

She begins her preparations by setting aside about an hour to read the two articles "All Children Can Write" and "Drawing Parallels: Real Writing, Real Reading," provided at the end of this section; and another hour to preview the tape itself. (The running time of "Time and Choice" is 23:09 minutes.) Because she wants to check the school equipment as well as the tape, Barbara decides to watch the tape at school.

Barbara wants to become familiar with the information on the tape, so initially she sets it up and watches it straight through. After watching the tape, she takes a few minutes to think about what she saw. She takes out paper and pencil and thinks about what struck her about the tape. What stuck out in her mind right away? She's pretty curious about that second-grade teacher's method of book choice. She sets the footage counter to mark these sections and watches it again. (See the section "Counters" in the chapter "Using Television and Videotape Effectively.")

Then, she decides to replay the tape, thinking about the teachers in her school and what might be most helpful to them. She remembers a conversation she had in the teachers' room a few days ago with several of the teachers. Some were talking about children choosing books during reading that didn't seem to be hard enough. Another wondered how she could read all the books her students might read if they didn't stick to the stories in the basal. Barbara decides that the notion of book choice and how the teachers could respond to the children's choices would be of special interest to the teachers who requested this workshop. She plays back those sections of the tape and programs them to replay at the workshop. (See the section "Auto-Search" in the chapter "Using Television and Videotape Effectively.")

It's clear that the different teachers on this tape are exploring different ways to work with their students to help with book choice and their response to literature. Barbara wants to include a time for the teachers at her school to discuss these different ways and brainstorm things they could try in their own classes.

She looks at the block of time she has to set up the workshop, then outlines the workshop as follows:

- **9:00:** Read a short piece to the whole group (from children's literature — maybe a fairy tale from Jane Yolen?). Ask for comments and questions on this piece of writing.

- **9:30:** Break into groups of three. Ask teachers to conduct these small reading-group conferences in a way that they might hold a writing-group conference, treating the book or article that they brought as what it is—a piece of writing. Directions to teachers: Please tell the group about the book or article that you have chosen to share, then read an excerpt from it—a favorite part, the lead, or a short chapter. Then, just as you would at a writing conference, take comments and questions from your peers. We'll take about 30 minutes for this—about ten minutes for each of you to share and get responses from your group members.

- **10:00:** Back into large group. Take a few minutes to lead a discussion on what people thought of that experience. Some possible questions: How did it work to talk about literature when everyone had read different pieces? Were you surprised by any of the comments made in your group? How has the discussion and sharing affected your appreciation of the book? What other books did you learn about that you might want to read? What did you learn about your peers that you didn't know?

- **10:30:** Show "Time and Choice."

- **10:55:** Ask the teachers to do a quick-write on their reactions to the tape. (Ask them, "What struck you?") About ten minutes.

- **11:05:** Ask the teachers to form groups of three again and share their reactions to the tape. (This will help set up future workshops based on the concerns and interests of the teachers.)

- **11:30–1:00:** Lunch break.

- **1:00:** Replay the sections of the tape dealing with book choice and teacher's response to children's reading. As a large group, brainstorm ways to handle book choice, responses to literature, and reading conferences that we might be comfortable with in the school.

- **1:45:** Ask the teachers to get into pairs to make plans for what their next steps will be. Set up what they are willing to try in each particular class, on the basis of one day a week at first, or whatever is comfortable. Group partners can help plan and provide ideas and, of course, support.

- **2:30:** Come together again as a group and share "the next step"—what each person intends to try. Ask each of the teachers to try to set up a time with their partners in a week or so to discuss how it is going, arrange a visit to the other's class, or in some way continue this feedback and support.

- **3:00:** Remind the teachers that the tape is available to view either at school or at home, if they prefer. Tell them about the articles available in my room that might be good resources to them. Give out copies of bibliography from handbook.
End of workshop.

Then, Barbara writes a letter to the teachers, asking them to bring something they are reading to the workshop:

To Workshop Participants:
Our workshop day is just around the corner, and as I finalize my plans for the day, I'd like you to do a little preparation, too. Think about some of the recreational reading you are doing now and plan to bring something you could share. I don't have any particular reading material in mind; it might be a novel, magazine article, poem, or anything else you care to bring.
I'm looking forward to Friday!

Sincerely,

Barbara

Barbara

This is one way of incorporating the tape into an in-service day. But what about a school that has considerably less experience with the writing process? Or one that has set aside less time to explore reading and writing connections? How could the tape be used at a school like this? One possibility is described below, for a three-hour workshop.

THREE-HOUR WORKSHOP

Dan is a second-grade teacher at a K–5 elementary school. Some of the teachers at his school have begun to teach writing as a process this year, beginning in the fall, when a five-week after-school workshop was held at their school for interested teachers. Teachers began to write during these sessions, and they continue to meet on a weekly basis to share their own writing, to talk about the progress of their students, and to iron out problems that arise in their writing programs. Now they have decided to both reinforce their knowledge of writing process and see how other teachers have begun to draw some parallels into their reading programs. After investigating their resources, Dan has agreed to act as leader in an after-school workshop using the "Time and Choice" tape.

Like Barbara, Dan sets aside about two hours of preparation time: first, to read the two articles "All Children Can Write" and "Drawing Parallels," and then to preview the tape itself. Because he has a VCR at home, it's most convenient for him to watch the tape there.

After an initial straight-through viewing, Dan thinks about how the teachers at his school might react to the tape. What will be the most helpful information for them? One thing that he noticed in the tape was the attitude of the children in the classrooms: they seemed excited about learning and genuinely involved in their reading and writing activities.

He is also struck by the many options available to children for topic choice, for working within the classroom, and for sharing the reading and writing activities. Reading and writing are closely allied in the school. It's something Dan and his fellow teachers need to think about as a staff. During the writing workshop, the teachers had explored their writing histories and discovered some of the roots of their feelings about writing and their implications for instruction. Dan decides that it might be helpful to begin with similar reflection on their reading/writing histories. Accordingly, he outlines his workshop as follows:

- **2:30–3:30:** Ask the teachers to brainstorm a list of their earliest recollections of writing in school as well as how they remember learning to read. After about five minutes, share these recollections in groups of three.

  Next, make a similar list of recollections of reading and writing in the middle- and high-school years, and again share in groups.

  Third, make a similar list of recollections since high school and share. Now, ask the teachers to select their three most memorable experiences about reading and writing—either negative or positive—and share these in groups of two. (These may have been shared before, but now they will be discussed as to their significance.)

  Last, pick the most significant one of the three most memorable recollections and quick-write on it for 10 minutes.

  Conduct a whole-group discussion on what we have learned about our reading/writing histories. How many have had times when they had combined reading/writing experiences? Brainstorm a list of the implications this has on how we teach reading and writing in our school.

- **3:30–4:30:** Read one or both of the articles from the package and get into groups of three or four to discuss them.

- **4:30–5:30:** View "Time and Choice." Quick-write to respond to tape. Share in groups. Decide what parts we might want to play back and focus on. Plan to follow up at next writing group.

  End of workshop.

OTHER POSSIBLE USES

The above are only two scenarios for the use of "Time and Choice: Key Elements for Process Teaching"; it can also be used effectively in a variety of other settings for both pre-service and in-service teachers. The tape can also be used to help explain your reading and writing program to parents, school board members, and even the students within your school. When you are deciding how to use this tape to best meet your needs, keep these things in mind:

- It is important to preview the tape before the workshop or course, in order both to familiarize yourself with it and to help you decide how it can be used to best meet the needs of its audience.

- It is essential to allow time for reflection after viewing the tape. Ideally, both a written response and peer discussion groups should be included in the workshop schedule.

- Provide time for viewers to plan how they might comfortably begin to incorporate some of the changes into their classrooms.

- The two articles included at the end of this chapter will give you and the workshop participants helpful background and theoretical information about the writing and reading process.

The Next Step

Once you have started using "Time and Choice" in your school, how can you and your staff continue to incorporate these ideas into your classrooms? There are several resources available to you:

1. Further reading material. See the annotated bibliography provided later in this section.

2. Further tapes in this series. "Time and Choice" gives you a broad overview of the philosophy of teaching reading and writing emphasizing process. Other tapes in the series provide a more in-depth view of these classrooms.

    "One Classroom: A Child's View" shows, among other things, a child's perception of the structure of her own classroom; her understanding of the reading and writing of the other children; a variety of environments within one classroom; and children as they engage in problem solving.

    "Writing Conference Principles: The Child Learns, The Teacher Learns" takes you into Pat McLure's writing class on a busy Monday morning and allows you to hear and see what the three children she confers with know about writing and about their topics; how Pat helps the children communicate that knowledge; how the writing conference can fit into the existing structure of a classroom; and how Pat analyzes these conferences.

3. Seek support from other professionals. If you are interested in finding out more about what further steps you can take, write to:

    > The Writing Process Lab
    > 106 Morrill Hall
    > Department of Education
    > The University of New Hampshire
    > Durham, New Hampshire 03824

Finally, and most importantly, you can also act as resources to each other, forming the kind of community of readers and writers as a staff that you would like to have in your classrooms. Many teachers find a weekly writing group essential for continuing support in their own writing, as well as for providing a forum in which to share successes and concerns about their students' progress. It's also helpful to visit each others' classrooms to see what's working well within your own school.

All Children Can Write

Donald H. Graves

Many children who have learning disabilities are poor writers. They equate their struggles in handwriting, spelling, and language conventions with a lack of ideas and information worth sharing. The writing-process approach to teaching first emphasizes what children know, then the conventions that will help them share their meaning with others in the class. This approach has led to major breakthroughs for young writers, particularly those who have learning problems.

This article reexamines writing as communication for oneself and for other audiences. This process occurs in classrooms where children see how teachers demonstrate their own learning in the midst of a highly structured environment.

Four essentials to a successful writing-process program are described: the adequate provision of time (at least 4 days per week), child choice of writing topic, response to child meaning, and the establishment of a community of learners.

Continued success in teaching writing depends on teachers' work with their own writing. Study programs, as well as additional reading materials, are suggested.

I stood at the side of Ms. Richards' third grade classroom watching the children write. We were at the beginning of our 2-year National Institute of Education study of children's composing processes. The school had diagnosed two of the children in Ms. Richards' room as having severe visual-motor problems. They were not hard to find.

Both leaned over their papers, their elbows crooked at right angles to their bodies to protect the appearance of their papers. I walked over to take a closer look at one of the two children's papers. Billy's paper was smudged, wrinkled, letters blackened; in several instances, his paper was thinned and blackened still more where he had gone through several spelling trials on the same word. The more serious aspect of Billy's writing profile was not his visual-motor difficulty, the appearance of his paper, or his numerous misspellings. Billy was a self-diagnosed poor writer. He connected his writing problems with a lack of worthwhile ideas and experiences. In addition, he was well-versed in what he couldn't do.

Billy had been in a separate program emphasizing visual-motor skills, letter formation, and various fine-motor tasks. No question, using a pencil was painful and arduous for him. Teachers complained that Billy rarely completed his work and was constantly behind the others, though he seemed to be articulate. Billy's program was skill-based, disconnected from meaning, and filled with positive reinforcement about his ability to form letters on good days. There was no attempt to connect his writing with the communication of ideas.

Children with learning disabilities often work on skills in isolation, disconnected from learning itself, and therefore disconnected from themselves

Source: From *LD Focus* 1(1) (Fall 1985), 36–43. Reprinted by permission of the author.

as persons. Therefore, like Billy, though their skills may improve slightly in isolation, the children do not perceive the function of the skill. Worse, they do not see the skill as a means to show what they know. Skills work merely supplies additional evidence for the misconception that they are less intelligent than other children.

Billy was in a classroom that stressed writing as a process. This meant the children received help from the time they chose a topic to the time they completed their final work. Ms. Richards played the believing game, starting with what Billy knew, particularly his experiences. In fact, Billy's breakthrough as a writer came when his teacher discovered his interest in and knowledge of gardening. As Ms. Richards helped him to teach her about this subject, she learned how to plant, cultivate, water, fertilize, and provide special care for certain varieties of tomatoes. Although Billy wrote more slowly than the other children, he became lost in his subject, forgot about his poor spelling and handwriting, ceased to cover his paper, and wrote a piece filled with solid information about gardening. Once Billy connected writing with knowing—his knowing—it was then possible to work with his visual-motor and spelling problems, but as incidental to communicating information.

Ms. Richards is now one of the thousands of teachers who teach writing as a process in the United States and the English-speaking world. New research and publications, university courses, and numerous summer institutes, are now helping teachers and administrators to find out for themselves what students can do when they focus on the meaning of their writing. Much of the focus of these institutes and courses is on the teachers' own writings: most of us had to rediscover the power of writing for ourselves before we could learn to hear what these young writers had to teach us.

Although writing-process work helps all writers, it seems to be particularly successful with people who see themselves as disenfranchised from literacy. I place in this group learners like Billy who have diagnosed learning disabilities and the accompanying "I-don't-know-anything" syndrome.

The writing-process approach to teaching focuses on children's ideas and helps children teach the teacher or other children in the class what they know, with emphasis first given to ideas and clarifying. This is the first experience many children have with other humans who work hard to point to what they know, instead of what is lacking in the message. Small wonder then that the writing process works best with the disenfranchised, who become a bit giddy at the prospect of seeing their words on paper affecting the thinking of others.

Understanding writing as communication is the heart of teaching the writing process. This article will first focus on the nature of writing, look in greater detail at research on the writing process itself, examine two principles in teaching writing, and then describe four basics in establishing a writing program. It also has a brief section on further reading and recommendations for summer programs for people interested in continuing their study of the writing process.

WHAT IS WRITING?   Writing is a medium with which people communicate with themselves and with others at other places and times. When I write, I write to learn what I know because I don't know fully what I mean until I order the words on paper. Then I see . . . and know. Writers' first attempts to make sense are crude, rough approximations of what they mean. Writing makes sense of things for oneself, then for others.

Children can share their writing with others by reading aloud, by chatting with friends while writing, and (in more permanent form) by publishing. Billy found that writing carried a different authority from spoken words. When he took the gardening piece out in December, he found that words written in September could be savored 3 months later. Furthermore, when he read the published books of other children in his room, he began to realize that his book on gardening was read by others when he wasn't present.

Written language is different from oral language. When Billy speaks, he reinforces his meaning by repeating words and phrases. Unlike when he writes, an audience is present; when the audience wanders or indicates disagreement, he changes his message with words, hand signals, facial expressions, and body posture. This is the luxury of oral discourse. "Error," adjustment, and experimentation are an expected part of oral discourse.

There is a different tradition surrounding most teaching of writing. Only one attempt, one draft is allowed to communicate full meaning (without an audience response). Red-lined first drafts are the norm; we blanche at any misspellings or crudely formed letters.

Still worse, writing has been used as a form of punishment: "Write your misspelled word 25 times." (This is called reinforcement of visual-memory systems.) "Write one hundred times, 'I will not chew gum in school'"; "Write a 300-word composition on how you will improve your attitude toward school." Most teachers teaching in 1985 were bathed in the punishment syndrome when they were learning to write. Small wonder that most of us subtly communicate writing as a form of punishment. We have known no other model of teaching.

THE WRITING PROCESS

When children use a meaning-centered approach to writing, they compose in idiosyncratic ways. Each child's approach to composing is different from the next. Some draw first, write two words, and in 10 minutes or less announce, "I'm done." Others draw after writing or do not write at all; instead, they speak with a neighbor about what they will write. Some stare out the window or at the blank page and write slowly after 20 minutes of reflection. At some point in their development, writers believe one picture and two words beneath the drawing contain an entire story. In the writer's mind, the story is complete; members of the audience shake their heads and try to work from drawing to text and back to understand the author's intent.

Such idiosyncratic approaches by children seem capricious to outsiders, confusing to children, and bewildering to us as teachers. We intervene with story starters to "get them going," produce pictures as stimuli for writing, and consult language arts texts for language activities. The texts provide "systematic" approaches, often through the teaching of the sentence, advance to two sentences, and finally development of the paragraph. Our detailed observation of young children writing shows they simply don't learn that way. Rather, they write three sentences in one in their first year, not understanding where one sentence ends and the other begins. Studies of children's understanding and use of sentences show they don't acquire full sentence sense until much later (about fifth grade).

The most pernicious aspect of teacher interventions is that children begin to learn early on that others need to supply topics because they come to the page with nothing in their heads. A focus on skills and form to the exclusion of child-initiated meaning further confirms their lack of fit with the writing process.

Prepared materials seek to reduce the stress and the uncertainty that writers face when they encounter the blank page. But the attempt to produce certainty through standardization by-passes the opportunity for child growth. There is good reason to expect tension when a child first writes.

When writers write, they face themselves on the blank page. That clean white piece of paper is like a mirror. When I put words on the page, I construct an image of myself on that whiteness. I may not like my spelling, handwriting, choice of words, aesthetics, or general cleanliness of the page. Until I can begin to capture what I want to say, I have to be willing to accept imperfection and ambiguity. If I arrive at the blank page with a writing history filled with problems, I am already predisposed to run from what I see. I try to hide my paper, throw it away, or mumble to myself, "This is stupid." But with every dangerous, demanding situation, there is an opportunity to learn. Teachers who follow and accompany children as they compose help them to deal with what they see on the page. The reason writing helps children with learning disabilities is that they do far more than learn to write: They learn to come to terms with a new image of themselves as thinkers—thinkers with a message to convey to the world.

TEACHING WRITING—TWO BASIC PRINCIPLES

After 12 years of working with writing research and the teaching of writing, I have found two principles essential for effective teaching of writing: (1) The teacher teaches most by showing how he/she learns, and (2) the teacher provides a highly structured classroom.

The best demonstration of how teachers learn is through their gathering of information from the children. They place the children in the position of teaching them what they know, usually through conferences. "Now you say that you have to be careful how deep you plant lettuce, Billy. Can you tell me more about that? And do you think the precise depth should be in your piece for the other children? Will they want to know that?" Billy's teacher has shown him how she learns and how he should learn to listen to questions he soon will be able to ask himself.

Ms. Richards, Billy's teacher, has a basic lifestyle of learning from everyone. Whether seated next to someone on a plane, in the teachers' room, or talking informally with children, she wants to be taught; in a lifetime she has learned how important it is to help others to teach her. People leave Ms. Richards' presence surprised they knew so much about their subjects.

Ms. Richards' classroom is a highly structured, predictable classroom. Children who learn to exercise choice and responsibility can function only in a structured room. Furthermore, the up-and-down nature of the writing process itself demands a carefully defined room. Predictability means that writing occurs daily, at set times, with the teacher moving in the midst of the children, listening to their intentions, worries, and concerns. They know she will be nearby attending to their work. She rarely addresses the entire class during writing time. She works hard to establish a studio atmosphere. Predictability also means she won't solve problems for them. Rather, she asks how they might approach the problem. She listens, clarifies their intentions and their problems, and moves on.

Children learn to take responsibility not only for their topics, content of their drafts, and final copy, but also for carrying out classroom decisions. A structured classroom requires an organized teacher who has set the room up to run itself. The teacher has already made a list of the things to be done to help the room function. From September through June, he/she gradually passes on those duties to the children. Attendance, caring for room plants and animals, room cleanliness, lunch lines, desk supervision, and cleaning are but a few examples of these delegations. When room structure and routine do not function well, the teacher and students plan together for the best way to make it function more smoothly. Ms. Richards' room is based on extensive preparation in room design and knowledge of materials, the children, and the process by which they learn to take responsibility.

Teachers who function well in teaching the writing process are interested in what children have to teach them. Writing-process teaching is responsive, demanding teaching that helps children solve problems in the writing process and in the classroom.

CARRYING OUT A WRITING-PROCESS PROGRAM

I am often asked, "What are the essentials to strong writing programs?" Although the list could be extensive, I think that if teachers understand the following four components, their writing programs will serve the children well. These components are adequate provision of time, child choice of topic, responsive teaching, and the establishment of a classroom community, a community that has learned to help itself.

Time

Our data show that children need to write a minimum of 4 days a week to see any appreciable change in the quality of their writing. It takes that amount of writing to contribute to their personal development as learners. Unless children write at least 4 days a week, they won't like it. Once-a-week writing (the national average is about 1 day in 8) merely reminds them they can't write; they never write often enough to listen to their writing. Worse, the teacher simply has no access to the children. He/she has to scurry madly around the room trying to reach each child. With little access to the children, the teacher can't help them take responsibility, solve problems for them, or listen to their responses and questions. The very important connection between speaking and writing is lost.

Although teaching writing 4 to 5 times a week helps the teacher, it helps the children even more. When children write on a daily basis, we find they write when they aren't writing. Children get into their subjects, thinking about their texts and topics when they are riding on buses, lying in bed, watching television, reading books, or taking trips. When they write regularly, papers accumulate. There is visible evidence they know and are growing. They gain experience in choosing topics and very soon have more topics to write about than class time can accommodate. Children with learning problems need even more time. They need to learn to listen to themselves with help from the teacher. In summary, regular writing helps:

1. Children choose topics,
2. Children listen to their pieces and revise,
3. Children help each other,
4. Teachers listen to child texts,
5. Skills develop in the context of child pieces,
6. Teachers to have greater access to children.

Topic Choice

The most important thing children can learn is what they know and how they know it. Topic choice, a subject the child is aware that he knows something about, is at the heart of success in writing. Billy struggled with handwriting and spelling and equated those problems with not knowing topics to write about. When his teacher helped him to discover his knowledge and interest in gardening, he began to write, first haltingly, then with greater flow. He was open to help with spelling and handwriting when he knew he had something to say. Skills are important; learning disabilities cannot be ignored, but neither can teachers or researchers forget that writing exists to communicate with self and others.

"How can I get the child to write? Do you have any good motivators?" are frequent questions asked of me in workshops. The word *get* embraces the problem. There are thousands of "motivators" on the market in the form of story starters, paragraph starters, computer software, animated figures, picture starters, and exciting "sure-fire" interest getters. We forget that children are very sophisticated consumers of motivators from Saturday morning television alone. Worse, motivators teach the child that the best stimulus comes from the outside. Writing actually demands dozens of motivators during the course of composing, but they are motivators that can only be supplied by the writer himself. All children have important experiences and interests they can learn to tap through writing. If children are to become independent learners, we have to help them know what they know; this process begins with helping children to choose their own topics.

Very young children, ages 5 through 7, have very little difficulty choosing topics, especially if they write every day. As children grow older and experience the early effects of audience, even under favorable learning conditions, they begin to doubt what they know. From that point on, all writers go through a kind of doubting game about the texts they produce. They learn to read better and are more aware of the discrepancy between their texts and their actual intentions. If, however, overly severe, doubting teachers are added to the internal doubts of the child, writing becomes still more difficult.

If children write every day and share their writing, we find they use each other as the chief stimulus for topic selection. If teachers write with their children, demonstrating the origin of their topics, and surround the children with literature, topic selection is even easier.

Topic selection is helped through daily journal writing where children take 10 minutes to record their thoughts. Teachers may also give 5- to 10-minute writing assignments, such as: "Write about how you think our room could be improved" (just following a discussion about how the room could be improved with the entire class) or "That upsets you? Well, blast away on paper with the first thoughts that come to mind. But write it for you; if you feel like showing it to me, okay." The teacher finds many occasions where it is useful to record thoughts and opinions on paper. Each of these approaches demonstrates what writing is for, as well as helping the children to have access to what they know and think.

Response

People write to share, whether with themselves or others. Writers need audiences to respond to their messages. The response confirms for the writer that the text fits his/her intentions. First, the teacher provides an active audience for the writer by confirming what he/she understands in the text and then by asking a few clarifying questions. Second, the teacher helps the entire class to learn the same procedure during group share time. Each writing period ends with two or three children sharing their pieces with the group while the group follows the discipline of first pointing to what is in the text, then asking questions to learn more about the author's subject. All of these responses, whether by the teacher or the other children, are geared to help writers learn to listen to their own texts.

While the children are writing, Billy's teacher moves around the room, responding to their work in progress. Here is an interchange Ms. Richards had with Billy about his piece "My Garden." (The child's text is presented, followed by the conference with the teacher.)

MY GRDAN
I help my Dad with the grdan ferstyou have to dig it up an than you rake an get the racks out of it. Than you make ros an you haveto be cerfull to make it deep enuff so the letis will come up.

Ms. Richards first receives the piece by saying what she understands about what Billy has written. She may also have him read the writing aloud to her:

Ms. Richards: You've been working hard, Billy. I see that you work with your dad on your garden. You know just what you do; you dig it up, rake it to get the rocks out, and then you have to be careful how deep you plant things. Did I get that right?

Billy: Yup.

Ms. Richards: Well, I was·wondering, Billy. You say that the lettuce has to be planted deep enough so the lettuce will come up. Could you tell me more about that? I haven't planted a garden for a long time.

Billy: Well, if you plant it too deep, it won't come up. Lettuce is just near the top.

Ms. Richards: Oh, I see, and did you plant some other things in your garden?

Billy: Yup, carrots, beans, turnips (I hate 'em), spinach (that, too) beets, and tomatoes; I like tomatoes.

Ms. Richards: That's quite a garden, Billy. And what will you be writing here next?

Billy: You have to water it once you plant it.

Ms. Richards: Then you already know what you'll be doing, don't you.

There are many problems with Billy's text: misspelled words, run-on sentences, missing capitalizations, and incomplete information. But Billy has just started writing his piece. Therefore, Ms. Richards works on word flow, helping Billy to know that he knows something about his subject and that he has a clear understanding of what he will do next. Later, when his piece is finished, she will choose one skill to teach within the context of his topic. Above all, she works hard to help Billy teach her about his subject, to keep control of the topic in his hands, no matter how uncertain Billy might feel about his subject.

Notice that Ms. Richards has spent no more than a minute and a half in response. She then moves to other children while responding in the same manner, receiving a text and asking questions. As she moves to different children in other parts of the room (she does not move in rotation or down rows; the movement appears to be random), the other children can hear that the teacher expects them to help her with what they know. Lengthy responses tend to take the writing away from the child. For example, if Ms. Richards were to say, "I had a garden once, Billy. I planted all kinds of things too: I planted cabbages, those same turnips, yellow beans, pole beans, and corn. Yes, it's hard work," she'd be identifying with Billy's garden and the hard work that goes into it, but *she* is now the informant. Such sharing should come only when his piece is completed and his authorship of this piece established.

Ms. Richards' statement is specific. When she receives Billy's text, she uses the actual words he has composed on the page. All writers need to know their words (the actual words on the page) affect other people. Notice that very little praise is given to Billy in this type of response. Instead, the listener, Ms. Richards, points with interest to the words; they are strong enough for her to understand and to remember them. The use of specifics, rather than the exclusive use of praise, is a fundamental issue in helping Billy to maintain control of his piece, as well as to take more responsibility for his text.

Establish a Community of Learners
Writing is a social act. If social actions are to work, then the establishment of a community is essential. A highly predictable classroom is required if children are to learn to take responsibility and become a community of learners who help each other. Writing is an unpredictable act requiring predictable classrooms both in structure and response.

Children with learning disabilities often have histories of emotional problems. Many have become isolated and feel very little sense of community. They themselves may produce unpredictable classrooms. Their histories in taking responsibility are equally strewn with failure. Notions of choice and responsibility are threatening and require careful work on a broad front. The following ingredients help to build a structured, predictable community of more independent writers.

1. Write daily, at the same time if possible, for a minimum of 30 minutes.
2. Work to establish each child's topical turf, an area of expertise for each writer.
3. Collect writing in folders so that writers can see the accumulation of what they know. Papers do not go home; rather, the collected work is present in class for student, teacher, parent, and administrator to examine. Some writing is published in hardcover or some more durable form.
4. Provide a predictable pattern of teacher participation by sharing your own writing, moving in the midst of students during writing time, and responding in predictable structure to your students' writing.
5. End each writing time with children responding to each other's writing in a predictable format: receiving, questioning.
6. Set up classroom routines in which you examine the entire day to see which responsibilities can be delegated to the children. Solve room problems in discussion. The group learns to negotiate, whether in working with a draft or solving a classroom problem.
7. Continually point to the responsibilities assumed by the group, as well as the specifics of what they know.

The writing classroom is a structured, predictable room in which children learn to make decisions. The external structure is geared to produce a confident, internal thinking framework within which children learn what they know and develop their own initiative.

Most teachers have been drawn into process work because they have seen significant personal growth by their students with learning problems. Students who lacked confidence and initiative and were disenfranchised from literacy learn to write, share their writing with others, and take charge of their own learning. Although some teachers may wish to start work on the writing process based on this article, I suggest additional reading and work with their own writing.

CONTINUING EDUCATION OF PROFESSIONALS

The single most important help to teachers who work with young writers is work with the teacher's own writing. Both the National Writing Project and our work here at the University of New Hampshire stress work with the teacher's own writing. Thus teachers become acquainted with writing from the inside by actually doing it themselves. It would be unheard of for a piano teacher, a ceramicist, or an artist working with water colors to teach someone their craft without practicing it themselves. Most of us have had little instruction in learning the craft of writing. We've written term papers, letters, and proposals, but we haven't worked with someone who has helped us to know what we know, then showed us how that knowledge is increased through the writing process.

I strongly encourage teachers to become involved in summer programs or consult their own universities to see if writing-process programs or courses are available. The following intensive summer programs concentrate on the teacher's own writing and the teaching of writing:

- Dean Timothy Perkins, Northeastern University, 360 Huntington Avenue, Boston, MA 02115
- Prof. Thomas Newkirk, English Department, Hamilton Smith Hall, University of New Hampshire, Durham, NH 03824
- Prof. Lucy Calkins, Teacher's College, Columbia University, New York, NY 10027

The National Writing Project has programs in almost all of the 50 states offering 3- to 4-week summer programs. Information about the National Writing Project is available from Dr. James Gray, National Writing Project, University of California at Berkeley, Berkeley, CA 94720.

For Further Reading
The following books will be helpful in acquiring more detail on teaching 9ting and organizing classrooms, as well as general background on learning and language theory.

Calkins, L.M. (1983). *Lessons from a child.* Portsmouth, NH: Heinemann.

Graves, D. (1982). *Writing: Teachers and children at work.* Portsmouth, NH: Heinemann.

Hansen, J., Newkirk, T., & Graves, D. (Eds.), (1985). *Breaking ground: Teachers relate reading and writing in the elementary classroom.* Portsmouth, NH: Heinemann.

Harste, J., Burke, C., & Woodward, V. (1984). *Language stories and literacy lessons.* Portsmouth, NH: Heinemann.

Newkirk, T., & Atwell, N. (Eds.), (1982). *Understanding Writing.* Chelmsford, MA: The Northeast Regional Exchange.

For teachers who wish to work with their own writing, I suggest the following:

Murray, D.M. (1983). *Write to learn.* New York: Holt, Rinehart, Winston.

Zinsser, W. (1980). *On writing well.* New York: Harper and Row.

FINAL REFLECTION

Before children go to school, their urge to express is relentless. They learn to speak and to carry messages from one person to another. They burst into their homes to tell what just happened outside. They compose in blocks, play games, mark on sidewalks, and play with pencils or crayons. For most children, early audiences are receptive: adults struggle to make sense of the child's early attempts to communicate.

When children enter school, their urge to express is still present. A few enter already scarred from attempts to communicate with others. But the urge to be, to make a mark on the universe, has not left them. As children grow older and spend more time in school, many become still more disenchanted with writing. They can't keep up with the rest of the class and equate their struggles with handwriting, spelling, and early conventions as evidence that their ideas are unacceptable and that they are less intelligent than others. Even for these children, the urge to express, to make worthwhile contributions, to express a meaning that affects others, does not go away.

The most critical factor for children with learning disabilities is the meaning-making question. Teachers need to first believe they know important information, then work overtime to confirm for the child the importance of that information. The children see their teachers write; they see and hear them struggle for meaning on an easel or overhead projector as they compose before them. The children become apprentices to the use of words.

When children write, they make mistakes on the road to communicating their messages. The teacher's first response is to the meaning. Before a piece is completed, the teacher chooses one skill that will enhance the meaning of the piece still further. From the beginning, the teacher works to build a strong history for writers through collections of all their work, some publishing, and the writers' effective sharing with other members of the class.

Most teaching of writing is pointed toward the eradication of error, the mastery of minute, meaningless components that make little sense to the child. Small wonder. Most language arts texts, workbooks, computer software, and reams of behavioral objectives are directed toward the "easy" control of components that will show more specific growth. Although some growth may be evident on components, rarely does it result in the child's use of writing as a tool for learning and enjoyment. Make no mistake, component skills are important; if children do not learn to spell or use a pencil to get words on paper, they won't use writing for learning any more than the other children drilled on component skills. The writing-process approach simply stresses meaning first, and then skills in the context of meaning. Learning how to respond to meaning and to understand what teachers need to see in texts takes much preparation.

The writing process places high demands on the teacher. The room is carefully designed for developing student independence: Decisions are discussed, responsibilities assigned and assumed. Routines are carefully established with writing becoming a very important part of the room's predictability. Initially, response to the child's writing is pedictable with receiving of the child's text, followed by questions of clarification, and the child's next step in the writing process.

Teachers who use the writing process to greatest advantage spend time working with their own writing. They read and become involved in many of the National Institutes that are helping teachers use writing as a tool for their own learning. Soon they find their students' learning careers change as well.

Drawing Parallels: Real Writing, Real Reading

Ruth Hubbard

At 11:00 A.M., the children in the sixth-grade class put away their writing folders. It had been a good writing session; the classroom hummed with the activity of a productive studio as students wrote, conferred in small clusters of their own choosing, and shared their writing when they needed an audience. Then, it was reading time. These self-directed writers now awaited Ms. Johnson's instructions.

"*Patterns* group, finish your vocabulary papers. *Reflections* group, do your glossary and reading questions. I'll meet with *Thundering Giants* first."

In marked contrast to the morning's writing session, only two students actually *read* at peak involvement during the ensuing reading time, and the children do not direct their own learning. Ms. Johnson is excited because her students are really writing during daily "writing time," but she is uneasy because these students are *not* really reading during "reading time."

She is enthusiastic about the independence of her students when they write, but uncertain how to transfer this same self-direction to their reading. Teachers who emphasize the process when they teach writing, are changing the philosophy by which they teach reading as well. How do teachers begin to incorporate this shift in philosophy into their teaching?

This question is the focus of a two-year research project at the Mast Way School, a K–5 elementary school in Lee, New Hampshire. Jane Hansen, Donald Graves, Ann Marie Stebbins, and I documented the way the teachers began to teach writing and reading as complementary processes during the 1983–1984 school year. They began by teaching writing as a process, and over the course of this first year, have drawn parallels between these two similar processes of meaning construction, writing and reading.

TIME

At Mast Way School, from the first day of school, the teachers set aside time for daily writing. In Pat McLure's first-grade class, for example, the children entered their room at 8:30 and went directly to their writing folders for thirty minutes of writing time. Then, in Pat's and in other classrooms, writing instruction was based on this real writing.

Setting aside time for writing is new, but schools have always planned large blocks of time for reading. Or have they? A recent study of elementary schools found that a very small percentage of time was spent in actual reading (Rosenshine and Berliner, 1978). In typical reading classes, sustained time for really reading books is sacrificed so that myriad reading "skills" can be taught. Bamburger (1976) studied several reading situations in an attempt to discover

Source: Ruth Hubbard, "Drawing Parallels: Real Writing, Real Reading." From Jane Hansen, Thomas Newkirk, and Donald Graves (eds.), *Breaking Ground: Teachers Relate Reading and Writing in the Elementary School*, pp. 175–81. Portsmouth, NH: Heinemann Educational Books, 1985. Reprinted by permission.

why some children read and others do not. His study concluded that children read both extensively and well when the main objective was to develop "joy in reading" through time to read real books. Those classes in which teachers concentrated heavily on reading skills did not produce readers who read widely or well. In effect, real reading was trivialized in these skills-oriented classes; students got the message that it was something to do after significant, important work was completed.

Second-grade teacher Leslie Funkhouser wanted to give her class time for reading real books, but wasn't satisfied when she tried Uninterrupted Sustained Silent Reading (USSR). Although her second-graders read every day after lunch in a twenty minute USSR period, their reading instruction was not based on these books. "Mastery Reading" skills sheets still comprised the "prime time" reading. But later in the year, Leslie began to make an effort to model her reading program on her writing class. She told her children they would begin "Reading-like-Writing Time" two days a week. On these days, the children's skills sheets were set aside; instead the children read trade books and stories of their own choice, and held individual and group conferences.

To parallel the instruction to writing time, Leslie began reading class with a quiet reading time, during which she circulated among the students in quick individual conferences. Then each day she would meet with a small group of readers. Just as in writing class, this flexible group was a mix of abilities. Instead of bringing stories they were writing, students brought stories they were reading. Each child read a small section of a book, and other group members made comments and asked questions, while Leslie recorded comments and questions that were asked, and wrote brief notes about the children's reading progress. What about the children not included in these conferences? They knew that during this time, two specific things were expected of them: to continue to read books, and to write an entry in their reading journals every day.

"I'll show you how we do our journals," Johanna explained to visitors one day. "What you do in a journal is you write the date of that day, and then you write down the book, and then you write down the author. Michael is doing a journal now. What he does is, he tells you the information about it, or how he likes it or what he doesn't like about it, or what's funny or sad, or whatever he wants to write about it. And then he puts it in his journal folder. . . . This is what people do after they do their journal: they keep reading, and they read chapter books or just books they want to read."

When reading time came to a close, the children volunteered to share their reading with the whole class, too, just as they shared their writing. By March, "Reading-like-Writing Time" expanded to a full five-day program. In this classroom, real reading has "prime time."

Pam Bradley, a fourth-grade teacher, was also unhappy that her students' reading time was not well spent. "I hate teaching reading the way I do." So she did something about it; she put into practice her own version of Atwell's system of responding to students' reading through journals. . . . In November, Pam and her students began to read trade books during reading time. Comprehension sheets were scrapped in favor of journals the children filled with comments about their own reading. Pam no longer corrected questions from a manual. Instead, she began to write comments and questions in the children's journals and to respond to their individual reading needs, as the following exchange shows:

November 18

Mike: When I start a book that I dislike I probly stop reading the book. What do you do when you start a book and you dislike it?

Mrs. Bradley: I guess I try to read a little more. Sometimes it gets more interesting. If it doesn't, I do not keep reading. There are so many other good books, I look for one.

November 20

Mike: The book that you read to us I thought it was good. I felt that Spinner's dad should of let the fish go because he is so big and Fish should live, too just like you and me. What do you think about the pitcher of "7 A.M. 1948"?

Mrs. B.: The picture reminds me of when my children were all small. I would be up early in the morning, and I'd be alone for a while, but knowing that any second they'd come barreling out of their rooms. It made me miss having little kids in my house.

November 21

Mike: I know what you mean because my aunt misses my two cousens because they're always out playing with their friends and going out on dates with there girl friends. The book that I am reading now is quite bouring to me so I took some of your advice but it still is bouring so I am going to get another book.

How is your book? What is your book about?

Mrs. B.: My book is about a lawyer who is trying to help a boy who is in trouble. I don't know yet if the boy really has broken the law or not. I hope he hasn't. You know, Mike, I love to read. I always have a book in case I have a few minutes of free time.

Pam and her students have time for real reading now, and time for genuine communication about the books they read. "When I corrected comprehension sheets, I just wrote with my arm," Pam Bradley told me in June. "Now, when I respond to the kids' reading in their journals, I write with my head and my heart."

CHOICE

From an environment that offers time to learn, children can make choices about what they need to support their growing literacy.

- "Hey, Jean, I know what I'm gonna write about today," Christine confided to her classmate. "My secret hiding place I go to to get away from my brother."

- "Did you notice I wrote 'One day' here? That's because it wasn't today, and it wasn't yesterday . . . It really was just one day," Jason explained to George and Cheryl as they wrote together.

- "I don't want to change it, though," six-year-old Renee told Andy, "and I don't have to, have to, have to."

Every day, these children learn to make choices in their writing, and they are conscious of their control over these choices—of topic, revision, illustrations. With this control comes commitment to and pride in their work. "Authority over writing belongs to the author," Donald McQuade (1981) states. "To usurp it wastes teachers' time." A successful writing program is based on choice: a successful reading program needs to open the same world of possibilities to children. Just as children who are taught to rely on assigned topics and story starters don't learn to take control of their writing, children who are constantly assigned stories someone else thinks they should read become passive readers (Maehr, 1976; Newkirk, 1982).

Choice of Books and Stories

Children need to read regularly from books they choose themselves. Pat McLure was confident that her first-graders could handle options and choices in their reading just as they do in their writing. "I'd like all of you to pick a book to read some time during this first working time," she told them. And they showed a range of strategies in the ability to choose appropriate books:

"What I chose was a book I could read that looks interesting," Andy explained to me.

"But how'd you know you could read it?" I asked.

"Well, I read a page. But I really didn't need to, 'cause I've read lots of *Clifford* books and I know they're a cinch."

Jeff chose *The Stunt Man*, by his classmate Nicky. "I chose Nicky's book 'cause he has good illustrations . . . Always!" Jeff told me he knew he could read it " . . .'cause all of the kids in this class write with words I know. Mostly anyhow."

David returned his first choice. "I didn't choose it any more," he explained. "Look at all the words on this page!" At last he hit on *The Popcorn Book* and contentedly settled down to read.

Leslie Funkhouser's second-graders handled their book choice a little differently. Brian, one of her students, explained to me that they know it's all right to read books of varying difficulty, and that they can identify books as hard or easy. "Well, we have different books we're working on. One could be pretty easy and we can go to it any time. We can choose one that's not too hard, but we need to work on a little more to read it, like there's some words we don't know. Then there's our goal book. That's one we really want to read and it's pretty hard."

Offering children book choices doesn't mean teachers have to throw away basals. Third-grade teacher Jan Roberts began to use the basal more as an anthology of stories, allowing the children choice in the stories and freedom in the discussions. She instructed her students to choose which story they would like to read and discuss. Just as in writing, the groups were based on interest instead of ability and the children ran the discussions themselves. As they read the stories of their choice, they wrote down comments and questions—things that interested them and they wondered about—to bring to their discussions.

Children in other classes too, could choose to read stories from the basals as well as trade books during reading time. There were multiple copies of these books, and the children often wanted to get together to talk about a story they had all read. Some students even monitored their progress by reading stories from increasingly difficult readers, proud of their accomplishment when they mastered a level which was once too hard for them.

Choices in Strategy

Book choices are not the only decisions real readers make. In characterizing the act of reading as recreating, Iser (1975) emphasizes this point. "We look forward, we look back, we decide, we change our decisions, we form expectations, we are shocked by their non-fulfillment, we question, we muse, we accept, we reject; this is the dynamic process . . ." (288). Pat McLure helped her students see the decisions they made when they read. "Well, you've all had a chance to look through your books," she began one day as she sat on the carpeted floor with three of her students. "Was anything hard for you?"

Christy shook her head vigorously. "No, I had trouble with this word, but I read the next page and figured it out."

Pat agreed, "That's one good thing you can do when you get stuck reading. Read on and see if you can figure it out."

Andy chimed in, "Pictures can help, too."

"Yes, they can. When you're reading, you use all the clues you can," Pat emphasized.

Later, Pat told me that she was excited that the children discuss the process they use when reading. And she had an explanation. "You know, it's because they're reading independently now and noticing how they're able to read. That independence and freedom is important so they'll continue to forge ahead."

When we make all the choices for our students, we lose the chance to explore new trails to learning with them, and they love the chance to explore. Leslie Funkhouser was surprised when seven-year-old Nathan chose a Beverly Cleary book and continued to read day after day this story far above his reading level. Discussions between the two showed that Nathan both enjoyed and understood this difficult tale.

"How is it that you can understand this book so well?" Leslie asked.

"Well, it's like this," Nathan explained. "I run my eyes down the page and look for conversation. I read that first 'cause it's easier. Then I have sort of an idea of what's happening and I can go back and figure out the other parts even when the words are hard."

Nathan's choice of strategies was an ingenious one, and one that works for him.

Choices in Meaning

Readers seeking meaning make choices. In fact, Rosenblatt (1983) contends that "reading consists of a continuous stream of choices on the reader's part" (124). Jan Roberts encourages these options when her third-graders have reading discussions. Jerry, Matt, Denise, and Joan had all read *The Great Houdini* and met to talk about it.

"I think the most important thing about the story was that the teacher cared—really cared—about his student," Jerry began.

Denise shot back, "Nope, I don't think so. I felt more like the teacher is better and wants to prove it."

"I thought the author was reminding us how dangerous the sea is," Joan announced. "And that you have to think about that when you're swimming."

"Yes, that makes sense," Jan Roberts agreed, joining the discussion. "And you may have been tuned in to that because you swim and compete. You know we've talked about how we all bring our personal experiences into our reading."

"I think the author wanted you to know that you can be whatever you want," Matt added.

Jan voiced her opinion, too, but not as teacher-leader; she was not offering her students "the correct" interpretation. "You know, I had a different idea. I thought it was more about learning about Houdini as a person."

Matt smiled, "So yours is the fifth idea."

"Yes."

The discussion continued with divergent interpretations of the story, the teacher offering her viewpoint, but as a "fifth idea." In the past, Jan Roberts' discussions followed the more typical basal pattern. But now, Jan's students have written for several months. They are used to choices and options in their writing and this has implications for the way she teaches reading.

"Last year, I would have pushed and pushed until they came around to my right answer. What a turn around! Now, I'm excited to see their minds going in a million directions. And because I know the kids, I can see that they make interpretations based on their experiences."

Because of the students' freedom to expand and explore rather than focus in on one narrow answer, discussions can take off in unexpected and rewarding directions.

Time passed quickly in Jan's reading class. The children put away their reading folders. It had been a good reading session; the classroom hummed with the activity of a productive studio as students read, conferred in small clusters of their own choosing, and shared their reading when they needed an audience. Jan smiled and echoed my thoughts when she told her class, "Well, folks, I think you're all set."

REFERENCES

Iser, Wolfgang. *The Implied Reader*. Baltimore: Johns Hopkins Press, 1975.

Maehr, M. L. "Continuing Motivation: An Analysis of a Seldom Considered Outcome," *Review of Educational Research*, vol. 46 (1976): 443–462.

McQuade, Donald. "Creating Communities of Writers." *Journal of Basic Writing*, (Summer 1981): 79–89.

Newkirk, Thomas. "Young Writers as Critical Readers." In *Understanding Writing*, T. Newkirk and N. Atwell, eds. Chelmsford, Massachusetts: Northeast Regional Exchange, Inc. 1982.

Rosenblatt, Louise. "The Reading Transaction: What For?" In *Developing Literacy*, R. Parker and F. Davis, eds. Newark, Delaware: IRA, 1983.

Rosenshine, B. V. and Berliner, D. C. "Academic Engaged Time." *British Journal of Teacher Education* 4 (1978): 3–16.

Bibliography

Calkins, Lucy M. *The Art of Teaching Writing.* Portsmouth, NH: Heinemann Educational Books, 1986.
  Calkins's book answers the question "What is essential in teaching writing?" The book takes the reader into real classrooms and examines different ways to help children with fiction, report writing, and poetry. She invites teachers of writing to explore different conference techniques and also discusses connections between the reading and writing processes.

Graves, Donald H. *Writing: Teachers and Children at Work.* Portsmouth, NH: Heinemann Educational Books, 1983.
  Graves shows teachers how to get a writing class started in this practical book for educators. He addresses the everyday concerns of practicing teachers who want advice on conducting teacher–student conferences, evaluating writing, understanding writing development, and keeping records on children's progress.

Graves, Donald H., and Stuart, Virginia. *Write From the Start.* New York: E. P. Dutton, 1985.
  Stuart and Graves show how parents and teachers can work together to help children write at home and to explore ways to improve writing instruction at school. They take you into classrooms from inner-city New York to mill towns in New Hampshire and show children who are learning the craft of writing. Practical advice for parents is included, as well as a helpful bibliography of suggested reading for both educators and parents.

Hansen, Jane; Newkirk, Thomas; and Graves, Donald (editors). *Breaking Ground: Teachers Relate Reading and Writing in the Elementary School.* Portsmouth, NH: Heinemann Educational Books, 1985.
  In this book, twenty practicing teachers and researchers write about how process approaches in writing can be used successfully in the teaching of reading. From their own classroom experiences, these educators show ways they have explored bringing together the teaching of reading and writing to help their students learn.

Murray, Donald M. *Write to Learn.* New York: Holt, Rinehart, and Winston, 1984.
  Through examining his own writing, author Donald Murray describes his model of the writing process: collect, focus, order, draft, and clarify. As the book unfolds, Murray takes the reader through these stages as he works on a piece about his grandmother, offering numerous approaches and techniques.

Newkirk, Thomas, and Atwell, Nancie (editors). *Understanding Writing.* Portsmouth, NH: Heinemann Educational Books, 1986.
  In this book, educators and researchers write about what they have learned and experienced as they taught writing as a process. Through observing, conducting research in their own classes, and trying out new techniques to solve problems as they arose, these teachers came to understand the writing development of their students. They share their knowledge with the reader.

Wells, Gordon. *The Meaning Makers: Children Learning Language and Using Language to Learn.* Portsmouth, NH: Heinemann Educational Books, 1986. Researcher Wells followed the development of a representative sample of children from their first words to the end of their elementary education. His book describes the pattern of development of these children and shows the active role that children play in their own learning. He also focuses on ways in which adults can collaborate with children in their learning to help them attain literacy.

The Writing Process Lab. Two collections of narratives are available from the Mast Way Reading and Writing Project:

- Volume I: *Children Who Write When They Read.* Durham, NH: Writing Process Lab, University of New Hampshire, 1984.

- Volume II: *Teachers and Learners.* Durham, NH: Writing Process Lab, University of New Hampshire, 1985.

One Classroom:
A Child's View

Data Sheet for "One Classroom: A Child's View"

Note: Zero counter when Heinemann logo disappears.

Segment No.	Beginning	End	Contents
1	00:00	1:52	Title, opening remarks by Donald Graves
2	1:52	2:10	Johanna's introduction and explanation of book area
3	2:10	3:06	Book coding and classification
4	3:06	3:41	Group reading conference
5	3:41	5:08	Journal proofing
6	5:10	6:32	Reading journals
7	6:32	7:07	Reading time
8	7:07	8:14	Reading other children's published books
		READING TRADE BOOKS	
9	8:14	9:06	Alexia: choose your own adventure
10	9:06	11:15	Jamie: book of poems
		WRITING	
11	11:15	12:42	Dana's mouse story
12	12:42	14:13	Skills sheet explanation
13	14:29	15:52	Writing together
14	15:55	16:34	Writing conferences

Suggestions for the Use of "One Classroom: A Child's View"

Classrooms that teach reading and writing by emphasizing the process as well as the product are growing in number. Teachers, researchers, and administrators are sharing their experiences with others. But there is another group of experts we need to hear and learn from—the children themselves. Because we wanted to learn about a child's view of her classroom, we asked Johanna Barmore to show us her room and how it works.

"I'm Johanna Barmore and I'd like to show you some areas today and this is Mrs. Funkhouser's room . . ." begins the tour of this second-grade classroom. And Johanna *does* show us several areas in her room—areas in which to physically work and learn, and also areas in our own teaching to think about. Because this tour is so rich in what Johanna shows us about an environment for literacy, the tape may be viewed many times, stressing different themes. It could therefore be included in workshops that cover different aspects of the reading/writing process. In this section, we offer some different ways you might focus on this tape. Although there are several ways to use this tape, it's important *always* to:

- Set aside time to preview the tape before the workshop, both as a learning experience for you, and so that you can use it to meet the needs of your audience.
- Read the literature in this section of the Resource Guide in order to give yourself valuable background information and to decide which articles will be the most helpful to your workshop participants.
- Include a time for response to the tape—either a written reaction or a group discussion. Better still, include both!
- Be sure to allow some time for the teachers to plan what their next step will be.

This resource guide is written to help teachers, administrators, reading specialists, writing coordinators, and other educators lead workshops in their schools or districts. The tape can be viewed individually as well, but it's still important to read this section of the Resource Guide and plan your response to the tape.

Each of the following workshops are planned to cover two hours, but they can also be used within longer workshops. These three workshops are on classroom structure, responsibility, and the role of the teacher.

WORKSHOP ON CLASSROOM STRUCTURE

A two-hour workshop on classroom structure can be organized and paced as follows:

1. Introduce the workshop (5 minutes).
2. Show the tape (20 minutes).

3. Break into three-person discussion groups (15 minutes).
4. Return to the large group to share findings (10 minutes).
5. Take a five-minute break. (This is optional.)
6. Read the Wells handout (20 minutes).
7. Conduct discussion (10–15 minutes).
8. Plan with partner (20 minutes).
9. Conclude the workshop (5 minutes).

"Social Structures" is a short piece written by Donald Graves in the midst of the second year of the Mast Way research project when he was gathering data in Leslie Funkhouser's second-grade classroom. To begin this workshop on classroom structure, read this piece aloud. (This should take about 5 minutes.)

Tell your audience that they will now be watching a twenty-minute tour of Leslie Funkhouser's second grade. Give instructions: "After this tape, you will be sharing your reactions in groups of three. Your discussion will be focused on these three things: What are the choices within this classroom? What are the boundaries within this classroom? And finally, what is revealed about what Johanna and the other children know about the classroom structure?"

Then, show the tape. (This will take around 20 minutes.)

Discuss the tape in groups of three as described above. (Take 15 minutes for this.) Provide handouts of the tape transcript (pp. 51–54) to help remind everyone of the contents of the tape.

Next, come back into a large group and create a composite list of the choices and limits in the classroom. (Take 10 minutes for this.)

If a break is to be included in the workshop, after this discussion would be an appropriate place. In a two-hour workshop, breaks are not always necessary. However, if you feel your group needs one, it's best to limit breaks to about five minutes.

Pass out the excerpt from Wells's book *The Meaning Makers* (pp. 65–71). Introduce the piece by explaining a little about the research it is taken from: "This is an excerpt from Gordon Wells's book *The Meaning Makers*. His book is based on a thirteen-year study, 'Language at Home and at School.' In the piece you will read, he discusses the problems with schools as environments for learning, then makes suggestions for creating a more collaborative structure, such as the room Johanna has shown us."

Ask the workshop members to take about fifteen minutes to read this piece to themselves.

After the reading time is up and you are sure all the participants have read the piece, lead a short discussion of some of the important concepts contained in the excerpt. You might ask questions about what concepts in the piece really struck them, what stood out for them, or what they could really identify with. It's often helpful to create a composite list on an easel or chalkboard.

After a short discussion—10 to 15 minutes—tell the participants to choose a partner for a planning period. Provide instructions: "As Gordon Wells stresses, there is no one formula for successful classroom management, but he does make several recommendations on how to begin to make changes in classrooms so that curriculum negotiation is possible. We are going to take about 20 minutes now to brainstorm and plan with a partner for a personal starting point—something you can plan now and start next week. Your partner should both help you plan something you can carry out and also set up a time to meet with you so you can both share how it's working and offer feedback to each other."

During this planning time, it is helpful for you as the workshop leader to circulate and offer a few comments to several partners rather than work exclusively with one other person.

After about 20 minutes, call the group back together and close the workshop by reading Leslie Funkhouser's advice to process teachers: "Recipe for Process" (pp. 57–58).

WORKSHOP ON RESPONSIBILITY

A two-hour workshop on responsibility can be organized and paced as follows:

1. Introduce the workshop (5 minutes).
2. Show the tape (20 minutes).
3. Do a quick-write (10 minutes).
4. Break into groups of four (15 minutes).
5. Return to the large group to share findings (10 minutes).
6. Take a five-minute break. (This is optional.)
7. Read handouts (15 minutes).
8. Plan in groups of three or four (10 minutes).
9. Return to the large group to share findings (15 minutes).
10. Conclude the workshop (5 minutes).

Begin the workshop by reading this quote by researcher Gordon Wells (from *The Meaning Makers*, p. 121):

> *When children have a feeling of ownership and share the responsibility for the tasks that they engage in, teachers find that their relationships with children change. Given responsibility, children behave responsibly and no longer have to be closely supervised every moment of the day. With an agreed agenda, they know what has to be achieved and spend their time productively, using resources appropriately, asking for the teacher's assistance only when other sources have proved inadequate, and moving on to a new task when the present one is completed. As a result, freed from the demands of managing resources, answering trivial questions about procedure, and continually monitoring classroom behavior, teachers are able to spend considerable periods of time with individual children, giving assistance when it is really needed and helping them to reflect on what they are doing and to see how to extend it in various directions.*
>
> *This, then, is the goal, and these are some of the benefits that are likely to result. But how can it be achieved?*

A good question! And one we'd like to focus on today. Leslie Funkhouser is a second-grade teacher who began to shift more of the responsibility for classroom management, and for learning, to her students. Through talking with her students, we found that we learned a lot about how the responsibility in the classroom is shared. Let's take a look at this tape now, which is a tour of Leslie's classroom conducted by one of her students, Johanna Barmore. Johanna shows us how all the members of their community share responsibilities, so that they all learn together.

Show the videotape. (This will take around 20 minutes.)

When the tape is completed, ask the workshop members to do a ten-minute "quick-write" on their impressions of the tape they just saw. (Allow 10 minutes for this.)

When they have finished, ask them to break into groups of four and share their responses. (Take 15 minutes to do this.)

Then, come back into a whole group and, together, list the responsibilities of the children on the tape (Allow 10 minutes for this.)

If a break is planned, now would be the best time for it.

Next, pass out copies of "Child Responsibility in the Classroom" (pp. 63–64) and "Experiment in Reading and Writing" (pp. 55–56). These two pieces were written during the two-year Mast Way research project and give a little more information about the responsibility of the children in the classroom. (Give the workshop members fifteen minutes to read these pieces.)

Next, ask the participants to get into groups of three or four and plan one thing that they do now for the children in their classrooms that they could turn over to the children. (Allow 10 minutes for this small-group discussion.)

Then, come back together into one group and share the things that the audience will be trying in their classes. As group leader, make a composite list, which you should then photocopy and give to all the group members. The participants should also now plan a time to get together and talk about how it has worked for them to begin to turn more responsibility over to the children.

Conclude the workshop by reading this quote:

> *A leader is best*
> *When people barely know that he exists,*
> *Not so good when people obey and acclaim him,*
> *Worse when they despise him.*
> *Fail to honor people*
> *They fail to honor you.*
>
> *But of a good leader, who talks little,*
> *When his work is done, his aim fulfilled,*
> *They will say,*
> *"We did this ourselves."*
>
> *Lao-tzu (604 B.C.)*

A two-hour workshop on the role of the teacher can be organized and paced as follows:

WORKSHOP ON THE ROLE OF THE TEACHER

1. Introduce the workshop (5 minutes).
2. Show the tape (20 minutes).
3. Break into groups of three (25 minutes).
4. Return to large group and share findings (5–10 minutes).
5. Take a five-minute break. (This is optional.)
6. Read Wells piece (15 minutes).
7. Create list in whole group (10 minutes).
8. Do a quick-write (10 minutes).
9. Share what's been written (10–15 minutes).
10. Conclude the workshop (5 minutes).

To begin this workshop on the role of the teacher in a process-oriented classroom, read aloud to the group the narrative "What We Do Here" by Lorri Neilsen, a researcher who spent time in Leslie Funkhouser's second-grade classroom. (This will take around five minutes.)

Then, introduce the tape: "From this short piece, you can see how important Leslie's role is in this classroom. It is, as she describes it, 'different —not less, but different.' We're going to watch a videotape that was recorded in Leslie's class. Although the tour is conducted by Johanna, a seven-year-old member of the class, it is through Johanna's eyes that we can learn a great deal about Leslie and her role in the classroom."

Then, show the tape. (It will take around 20 minutes for this.)

Afterwards, pass out copies of the transcript of Johanna's tour, and give the following instructions: "Go through this transcript now and asterisk three things that really struck you on the tape. Then, in groups of three, make a composite list of those stars items." (Take 10 minutes for this.)

"Now, with your group, decide how the teacher's role affected the things that you've listed. In each of these instances, what do you think Leslie did to make that possible?" (Take 15 minutes for this.)

Then, come back as a whole group and share the responses. (Allow 5–10 minutes for this.)

At this point, if a 5-minute break is planned, take it.

Next, pass out copies of the extract of Gordon Wells's book *The Meaning Makers* (found on pp. 65–71) and instruct the group to take about 15 minutes to read it carefully.

Then, as a whole group, make a list of characteristics of the role of a teacher in a process classroom (based on what has been learned both from the tape and the Wells handout). After at least six or seven items are listed and have been discussed, instruct the group as follows:

"Now, go through this list and mark for yourselves what you consider to be the three most important items. We're going to take 10 minutes to quick-write ways you fit into this role and how you can build on what you already do." (Allow 20 minutes for this activity.)

After this writing exercise, ask for two or three volunteers to share what they have written, either by reading their quick-write or by explaining it orally. (Take 10–15 minutes for this.)

Conclude the workshop by reading this quote by Giamatti from "The American Teacher" (*Harpers*, September 1980, p. 24):

Teaching is an instinctual act, mindful of potential, craving of realizations, a pausing, a seamless process, where one rehearses constantly, sits as a spectator at a play one directs, engages every part in order to keep the choices open and the shape alive for the student, so that the student may enter in, and begin to do, what the teacher has done: make choices.

Transcript of Tape: Johanna's Tour

Johanna: I'm Johanna Barmore and I'd like to show you some areas today and this is Mrs. Funkhouser's room: Room Nine at Mast Way.

This is, right over here, this is like the book area. And right here is where we code the books, and how we code it is we put what it is, and then we put a dot here. And then we put that color dot on each of those kinds of books. Like this is a mystery story book, so we would have a dark blue dot on each of the mystery stories and we put it in this container. (This one isn't supposed to be in the mystery books, but . . .) And so, so then you know where to put it back when you're finished with reading it.

And then these are the hard-covered books that you can read, and then these here are published books. We publish these books so that the whole class can read them instead of having to ask you.

And right over here is where they're sharing. This is where people share, and they're reading stories, like Jennifer's reading a story right now. And she's reading *The Circus* and then people ask her questions after she's finished reading it and then you go on to another person . . . And Mrs. Funkhouser, she puts down the books that they're reading and she also puts down the author and the name. And she also puts down who else is sharing and she puts down the questions that she wants to ask.

Now I think I'll show you how they proof journals.

This is Karen. She's proofing a journal. (Can I lift this up for a second, Karen?) See, this is the sheet that you have. If there's a word that you spelled wrong, you circle it. If there's a capital letter that you didn't make it capital, you'd put a square around it. If there's periods and question marks that you forgot, you put a line under it. And if there's size of letters or backwards letters, you put two lines on it. And if it's not an incomplete sentence, you write an *I*, a *C*, and then cross it with a line. And then, right here, is spelling to check and that means you write down the spelling words that you got wrong. And you put 'em down the way you writ them and then you find out what the real way is to spell 'em and you spell that next to them. And the way you find out how you really spell them is in a dictionary, the book you read, or a friend. But the friend you should do last. And then "other skills" is what other things you missed. You write down what other things you missed.

And now I think I'll show you how we do our journals.

Michael, he's doing a journal right now. What you do in a journal is on the paper it says "date" and you write the date of that day that you do that journal, and then it says "book." Wait. Can I see this? See the date? And then it says "book." And then he writes down the book. And then it says "author," so he writes down the author. And they leave an extra line here so that if you can't put the whole title on one line, or anything on one whole line, you can put part of it on the second line. And then what he does is he tells the information about it or he tells how he likes it, or how he likes it, or what he doesn't like about it, or that's funny, or sad, or whatever he wants to write about it. And then he puts it in his journal folder, and you have to do one each day unless you're sick or something and—or unless you have to do something special for the teacher, and so that's what you do when you do a journal.

This is what people do after they've done their journal. They keep reading until writing time. And they read like chapter books or just books they want to read. And three people are to one place at a time, unless they're being very quiet. And you can also read with a friend if you want. And you can—well, actually, you can read with two friends if you want, so, but you can not read with three friends because that would include four people.

And now I think I'll take you to somebody reading a published book.

Here's Derrick. He's reading a published book that four people made. It has a lot of pages in it, and they made their own pictures, and so it has four stories with four girls in it. No. Yeah, four stories with each story has four girls in it. And each story has a mystery in it. And on each story somebody finds a treasure. They always, always find a treasure. Sometimes it's a big mystery. Sometimes it's a little mystery, and at the end of this book they get the biggest, biggest treasure in the world.

And he's also read one, I think, or he's about to read one. It's *The Thanksgiving Book* by Jason Peters. He's moved, but his books are still here.

So, OK, this is Alexia and she's reading a book. It's called *The Haunted House*. It's a Choose-Your-Own-Adventure. Choose-Your-Own-Adventure is where you start on the first page and go to the second page. And on the second page it has a choice for you to do. You can either go to someplace or you can go to a different place. And so you pick one of those and then you go to that place, and it says the page number that it's on. So then you go to that page number. And then it tells you to either go to a certain page or it has more questions in it. And there's lots of stories in there, like 8 or 9 or 10. They're pretty small and you could —you're always on a different adventure each time unless you've read all the adventures, and you have to go through another time.

And this girl over here. She's Jamie. She's reading a poem book. It's called *Where the Sidewalk Ends*. And it has lots of little poems. They may be big poems sometimes. Some of the poems are funny. Some of them aren't funny, and some of them are sad. Like there's a sad one that's called "Sister for Sale" 'cause he's selling her sister. But the rest of them are pretty funny. Like "Band-Aid Aides." This kid right here (I'll show —can I show the picture, Jamie?)—he has band-aids all over him. And (can I read it?) it goes like this:

> *I have a band-aid on my finger,*
> *One on my knee and one on my nose.*
> *One on my heel and two on my shoulder.*
> *Three on my elbow and nine on my toes.*
> *Two on my wrist and one on my ankle.*
> *One on my chin and one on my . . . chin.*

No, wait. Ask Alexia.

Alexia: I can't see it—it's upside down . . . "Thigh."

Johanna: Thigh.

Four on my belly and five on my bottom.
One on my forehead and one on my eye. (OK, where was I?)
One on my neck. And in case I might need 'em,
I have a box full of thirty-five more.
But, oh I—do think, it's sort of plenty,
I don't have a cut or sore.

OK. And that's one of the poems. And then there's one of the poems that's "A Man's Beard," and it tells about a man who doesn't wear any clothes cause his beard. His beard is so long that it can cover him up. So, that one's a very, very short one. Well, let's go somewhere else now.

OK, What Dana's doing is she's writing a story. Now, you don't have to write a story by using plain paper and writing lines on it. You can also use lined paper, but she, I guess she wants to do a story with lines of her own. And this story is called (what's it called?) "A Mouse Story." It's about a mouse family. I know a little bit about it because Dana's told me a little about it. And about it is, a part of it, a mouse—a mouse family goes on a picnic and one of the mouses gets smushed. And, so, she's, it's a pretty long book so far and she's also done lots of other books this year and she's about finished with this, right Dana? And she's got, she's got a lot of words on it. Um, um. Maybe she could read it right now. Want to ask her that? OK. She doesn't want to. She's got other stories in here and she's got a skills sheet. (Can I take these out and show them the skills sheet?) This skills sheet shows her skills. It's a skills sheet. And there's like one skill that you should know is "My Daddy and I," and capital letters, and beginning of sentences, names, I, days of the week. And then there are words down here that are words that you should know. Like "when," "what," "are," "saw," "they," "was," "eat." And then, "Skills I Know." She knows. No—no. "Skills I Know"—she hasn't written anything down there because we don't have to. Then "Skills to Learn." And she's learned a skill there that's question mark? I don't know what that is because it's in cursive. Quotation marks. Well, it's quotation marks and she learned that at that date. And so that's her skills sheet that she has stapled on there. And some people, they write down the stories that they've written. Oh, she's about to start on a new story 'cause she's done with the mouse story. And I think I'll take you to two people that are reading together.

OK. These two people are writing together. This is Jennifer and this is Sheryl. Jennifer is reading about a book that's on her friends. Friends are . . . (Can I see your friends, Jennifer?) They're Dana, Sheryl, Johanna, Alexia, Monica, Karen, and Sarah and Jamie. And Mrs. Funkhouser. And it was illustrated by her, too, and it was also written by her. It's a very long story and the beginning of telling about each friend there's a picture of her and that friend. And, uh, Sheryl, she's—can I show this?

Sheryl: I don't care.

Johanna: She's writing about her boyfriend. And she's written about him once before but she's writing about him again because she didn't like that story about him. So, that's what she's doing. And these two are writing together because you can write together. You can have three people writing together at the most. And that's all you can have writing together. But they're just two people writing together. They just decided to have two. So, let's go somewhere else.

OK. These three people. Mrs. Funkhouser—Well, these two are talking, writing the same story together and Mrs. Funkhouser is talking about it with them and she's asking them questions. And, as I told you in writing, with the, reading slip, she's doing the same thing with them except there's no other people in the group. And she asks them questions, and they also tell her about it, and they also read her the story.

This is what the room is like, and I am glad to have you to tour you around this room and show you about reading and writing. This is Johanna Barmore, and—goodbye!

Experiment in Reading and Writing

Leslie Funkhouser

"I'm working with Andrea," explains Emily. "She's shy but very nice. The first time she didn't want to read so I read a book to her. Then this week Mrs. Damon told her to read from her writing book to me. Their books aren't like ours. You see, they are just learning words and put down mostly letters. Their books don't have titles like ours either. But Andrea can spell and read 'cat' and 'dog.' "

"What will you do next week, Emily?" asks Heather.

"I'll bring a book to read to Andrea but I don't want to push her to read yet."

"When do you think a teacher should push, Emily?" asks Ms. Funkhouser.

"Well, it will take awhile. She needs to get used to me. Then maybe we can make a book together of pictures or things she knows. I think she knows 'ball' too. Do you think I should spell words for her? Like if we drew a ball and she only knew 'B' should I tell her 'all'?"

"Maybe that would be something to talk over with Mrs. Damon," responds Ms. Funkhouser. "What do you think?"

"OK, sounds like a good idea."

"Emily is shy, too," Alisha explains with more excitement then I've ever seen. " 'Adopting is Kindie' is a lot of fun. Emily wrote about rainbows twice and read her stories to me. She likes rainbows a lot. So do I, so we might write a story together about them."

"Were her stories the same or different?" asks Jamie.

"They were a little different but had some colors the same," Alisha explains.

"I had some problems, Miss Funkhouser. I don't have enough to do for the whole 15 minutes," says Andy. "Also, David doesn't want to do what I tell him. I suggested that we pick out a book to read together but he didn't want to. I don't think I did very well with him today."

"Maybe you can bring David to our room next week, Andy, and I'll help you both work it out."

"OK. Great, Miss Funkhouser. That will be good."

"We're reading over Daniel's stories to think of other topics he can write about," explains Josh as I arrive in the kindergarten to see how things are going. "He wants me to help him make a topic list. Before I have to go I hope to help him get two or three topics down in his book. He'll then have ideas for more stories."

Source: Leslie Funkhouser, "Experiment in Reading and Writing." From *Teachers and Learners: A Collection of Narratives from the Second Year of the Mast Way Reading/Writing Research Project*, pp. 104–106. Compiled by Ruth Hubbard and Dori Stratton. Durham, NH: Writing Process Lab, University of New Hampshire, 1985. Reprinted by permission.

As I arrive back at the cubby where Josh and Daniel are working after checking on Eddie, Daniel tells me that he will write a story about his pet rabbit next.

"Josh thinks this will be a good story," he states. "I like Josh to help me with my stories. He's a real good helper."

"I was excellent!" shouts Michael as he arrives back in our room on Friday. "I read two books, *Tim* and *Al* to Sevey and she really liked them. I didn't miss any words, either!"

Andy is so excited that he is pacing back and forth. "I go to the kindergarten in ten minutes. How long are we going to keep doing this, Miss Funkhouser? I hope until the end of the year! I just love it!"

Seth shares about his two experiences helping Jeremy with writing.

"I didn't realize how good I was at reading and writing until I had to help teach someone else. I've gotten much better this year."

These bits and pieces of conversations during the past two weeks are outcomes of Florence Damon's kindergarteners' and my second graders' most recent experiment. Each of my students has adopted a kindergarten child to help with either their reading or their writing. One day a week for about 15 minutes they work with their "adopted kindies." My students are responsible for planning what they will do, keeping their appointment, and sharing with their classmates how it went. So far, their comments have been very enthusiastic and they think it's great.

Recipe for Process
Leslie Funkhouser

Serves up to 25.

FILLING:

- Ability to Negotiate
- Choices
- Extended Time
- Listening
- Boundaries
- Shared Responsibilities

BOUNDARIES:

Mix one adult and up to 25 students.
Discuss the importance of boundaries to insure a learning environment for
  all.
Set up rules together.
Limit these to four or less.
Try them out.
Discuss their importance as the year progresses.
Refrigerate if not needed.

SHARED RESPONSIBILITIES:

Think about all the jobs that you do in one day during school time.
Can any be delegated to children?
At first, relinquish calm, efficiency, and perfection.
Teach the children about the job.
Help them if they need help while learning.
Cook on low for about five weeks and you will begin to ask yourself, ''Why
  am I here?''

ABILITY TO NEGOTIATE:

We as teachers often need answers to daily dilemmas . . . the pokey worker,
  the talker, the child constantly seeking attention. The children often have
  good solutions for our daily problems. Consult them for advice. They can
  learn that a smooth day means help from *all*.
Listen in . . . they negotiate contracts with one another constantly.
Remove from heat when boiling stage is reached.

Source: Leslie Funkhouser, ''Recipe for Process.'' From *Teachers and Learners: A Collection of Narratives from the Second Year of the Mast Way Reading/Writing Research Project*, pp. 97–98. Compiled by Ruth Hubbard and Dori Stratton. Durham, NH: Writing Process Lab, University of New Hampshire, 1985. Reprinted by permission.

CHOICES:

Mix a combination of possibilities with a few of your high expectations.
Discuss why it is necessary to self-evaluate frequently.
Provide extremes to insure success for all and challenge for all.
Work hard each day to learn more about each child's decisions.
Save a dash of "no" for times your mixture begins to break down.

LISTENING:

We all need to know a good listener.
Listening is hearing another's tales, feelings, ideas, and questions.
It does not involve evaluation, judgement, or agreement.
Your response is merely a clarification of what you heard.
Your questions are tools for gathering more information.
Ice with a smooth stroke so that the recipient feels proud and deliciously
topped.

EXTENDED TIME:

Fight to block out the guilt and worries about the curriculum to cover, dead-
lines to meet, benchmarks in the year to prove student competencies.
Live each day as if it were the most significant in the year.
Flavor with laughter.

Mix together, risk, fail, think about what you've learned. Share your knowledge with others!

Social Structures

Donald H. Graves

While reviewing the data for the first half year in Leslie's room, I was surprised by how much Leslie works on developing a society in her classroom. By society, I mean how much she works on the ways in which the people in her room live and work together. Since she sees reading and writing as something to be shared, as well as developed for personal thinking and enjoyment, it is only logical that extra effort would go into the social side of things.

None of what I have found is new. Every teacher has to work on room structure, responsibilities, and work habits. Maybe the part that is new to me, is in seeing their direct linkage to an effective reading and writing classroom. Let me be specific.

Back on September 7th, Leslie stated to Jane, "Children need to learn who to talk to about their subjects." A simple statement, yet subsequent data show that that statement of learning theory had enormous implication for social structure within the room. Children in that kind of room are going to have to have access to each other, learn what each other knows, and learn how to help each other. At the end of last year we had Johanna Barmore take us on a tour of the room. One of the inescapable bits of data was her ability to tell about the content of other children's current and old writing pieces. Not only that, but she knew who to seek out for help if a piece of reading was giving her difficulty.

Leslie takes her demonstrations of literacy seriously. The very first week of school she shared her reading of *Time* magazine, and showed how to choose books from the book area. She shows how she chooses books and composes some of her pieces. She does this because she wants to demonstrate the kinds of thinking that go into responsible choice for both reading and writing. Even though our research focuses on the reading and writing, Leslie works still harder at dealing with the consequences of choice.

The tough part about choice is in making good decisions. Some children don't choose their books well and have to have a swap week, a week in which Leslie chooses two books and they choose one. My research focus was on those data, but as I look things over the greater teaching was at the point of children taking each other's books. Back in September Ned came unglued when Allan took Ned's book to read, simply because he wanted it. For a moment it was hard to believe that Ned wasn't telling a good story because he was the usual aggressor. As it turned out, Ned was right.

For about ten to twelve weeks Allan functioned in that room as a kind of intellectual pariah. Rules weren't for him; if he liked a book he took it; in discussions he'd simply butt in, not waiting his turn. Allan was a well-read child who knew more about the content of other people's pieces than the authors usually knew themselves. He was the self-designated expert on pre-

Source: Donald H. Graves, "Social Structures." From *Teachers and Learners: A Collection of Narratives from the Second Year of the Mast Way Reading/Writing Research Project*, pp. 87–91. Compiled by Ruth Hubbard and Dori Stratton. Durham, NH: Writing Process Lab, University of New Hampshire, 1985. Reprinted by permission.

historic animals. Other children had to see him about their writing or reading if they chose that area. But he used his consultancy to maintain control of his turf; he rarely gave actual help.

The other day Ruth overheard Allan helping Mickey with something he was writing. He hadn't spelled "people" correctly. But Allan said to Mickey, "Well, you can read it the way you've spelled it. You are coming along very well." Allan has now become a classroom leader from the standpoint of giving help that really is help; he listens to what they say, and extends their work, often making personal comments on the progress of their efforts.

Back to Ned. Yesterday morning Ned came in with a child magazine featuring "Leaping Lemurs" from Madagascar. He negotiated with Leslie about finding out more information about them. When he got the green light, he charged over to the chalkboard where children were signing up for library. The rule states, "No more than three children out of the room at one time." Allan, Sandy, and Nick had already posted their names on the chalkboard and were gathering notepaper and other books preparatory to leaving.

What Ned *didn't* do was significant. He didn't attempt, as in the past, to erase a name from the board and replace it with his own. He continued to negotiate with Allan and Sandy. "Come on, let me go first; I won't be gone long," begged Ned. Sandy, who wanted to start working on another type of endangered species, just nodded a negative. Sandy, an expert in self-interest, combined Ned's with his own: "I've got an idea, Ned," said Sandy. "You let me know what kind of books you want and I'll bring them back to you." That seemed to placate Ned. At the same time, the wise Sandy knew he'd get more time of his own in the library, and less time writing in his reading journal. All of these negotiations over turf, rules, and continued work in reading were all conducted without the teacher present.

Role reversals are also important. Not only does it give children practice with giving assistance, but it also gives them the understanding that they can solve problems. If a teacher consults them, the implication is they possess information that can be used to solve problems by themselves. And all of this has much to do with their own sense of independence, as well as what they have to offer to the classroom. Counter to most educational expectations, particularly in the adolescent years in American education, Leslie's children have responsibility for themselves and for others. Children work together and when there are problems it is a time for room concern.

If children had total control for decision making and chose all books and topics, they'd quit school tomorrow. In fact, a kind of anarchy would prevail that might make teachers quit before the children. Not everything is up for discussion or choice. It can't be. Peremptory "no"s frame in the band of choice and decision making. "You *will* read; you *will* write; you *will* go outside at recess. Only three people are to be at the library at one time." And decisions are firm.

Elaborately defined territories and accomplished social negotiation lead to good use of time by the children. During reading/writing time yesterday morning, I noted a 90% on task time with children either reading or writing *without specific direction* by the teacher but with very carefully defined guidelines developed since September. Independent work in September, particularly from the third week until the fourth in October, was not nearly what it is today. In the first hour and one half yesterday morning, Leslie only spoke once to the entire class, and that was to bring children to the table who wanted to publish their "endangered species" reports. Sandy wasn't going to come, but Leslie directed him to attend because "I need you to share information on the wolf.'' He had done some good work and she thought it might be helpful to the other children. Again, the social structure is one where a teacher preempts individual choice if he has something that may help others.

We are finding that the necessary social frameworks, which operate in any room, *can* be created to complement children's learning as they read and write.

What We Do Here

Lorri Neilsen

"So, are you getting pretty used to it by now?"

Ruth and I stifled a laugh and Leslie smiled broadly. We were in a circle, the second-grade students, Leslie Funkhouser (the teacher), Ruth Hubbard, and me. Leslie had introduced herself to the students, saying that she had taught primary school for several years in other New Hampshire schools. She was beginning the circle introductions, demonstrating how we introduce ourselves as we sat together the first morning back at school.

It was Nicky, sitting beside Leslie, who first responded to the brief history of her teaching career. "So," he said, "Are you getting pretty used to it by now?"

Perhaps we were amused at Nicky's comment because it was precocious, because it sounded so much like the "phatic" communication we use when we are first introduced to someone and, adopting a friendly and interested tone, we smile and say, "So, how have you enjoyed it so far?"

But Nicky's comment was a demonstration of the power of demonstrations. Children watch us as we speak; they pick up more than the words we use—they pick up the context, the appropriateness, the tone, everything. We demonstrate; they emulate. To use a sociolinguistic term, they are becoming communicatively competent. Perhaps we laughed because Nicky not only knew exactly what to say, but also when and how to say it. We laughed because it was perfect.

Demonstrations are the center of Leslie Funkhouser's classroom. With her tone of voice, her relaxed smile, her calm and assured demeanor, she demonstrated to the children how they will communicate to her and to each other.

When Leslie sat down to read silently ("No interruptions for ten minutes, please"), she demonstrated the value she placed in being able to spend time alone with a book. When she held up three choices for herself for quiet reading and explained to the children how and why she chose each of them, she demonstrated her interest in reading widely and from various levels of "difficulty."

But these examples are only a few of the hundreds of details that paint the picture of school for the second-grade students in Leslie's room. The way the room is set up—the library, the published books, the author's chair, the group tables, the typewriter, the author of the month—all contribute to Leslie Funkhouser's demonstration of the value she places in reading and writing and the enthusiasm she holds for the children's learning. Leslie is her room; Leslie is the demonstration.

It was shortly after ten o'clock, just before recess. The children were all reading, discussing their books with each other, or signing out or back from the library.

School had been in session for only an hour and a half but you could tell—they were getting pretty used to it by now.

Source: Lorri Neilsen, "What We Do Here," From *Teachers and Learners: A Collection of Narratives from the Second Year of the Mast Way Reading/Writing Research Project*, pp. 1–2. Compiled by Ruth Hubbard and Dori Stratton. Durham, NH: Writing Process Lab, University of New Hampshire, 1985. Reprinted by permission.

Child Responsibility in the Classroom

Donald H. Graves

I knew that Leslie's room involved a highly cooperative system of taking responsibility for the way the classroom ran. It wasn't Leslie's room as much as it was their (teacher/child) room. Classroom problems were problems for both teacher and child.

Process classrooms require structure. Structure helps children to take responsibility, to see how their tasks contribute to the room harmony. Children learn to handle responsibilities their way but within a framework that allows for individual interpretation as to the best way to carry it off. That same framework is applied to interpretations in reading and writing. Children have responsibility for textual interpretation, for choice of topic or book, yet there are firm guidelines with some latitude for child variance in process.

Although I am generally aware of how Leslie consciously delegates tasks in the room, I finally popped these two questions: "What kinds of jobs do your children handle by themselves? What I'm getting at is: how many things do your children do where they don't have to consult you?" And here is her response:

1. They pass out the papers at the end of the week. I used to have a large basket over by the board. The basket filled up with papers that went home weekly. But now that I have the folders, that doesn't really happen so much any more.

2. Library job: Someone keeps the books in order for a week. They check the codes of the books to make sure they are in the right place.

3. Messenger: Any message to be taken to the office or other teachers. Weekly job.

4. Milk tickets: One child goes to get milk at snack time. Weekly.

5. Boards: Wash the boards at the end of the day if there is anything on them needing cleaning. Weekly.

6. Hall checker: See if children's behavior is OK in the hall. Children who don't use the halls well will get a warning from that child. Weekly.

7. Tapes: Handle signups in the listening area. Don't really need this job as much now as the children don't use that area much. Just use the area on their own. Weekly.

8. Taking attendance: Weekly.

9. Checking desks: Every Friday the children's desks are cleaned. This person goes around and passes on the cleanliness of the desks in the room. Weekly.

Source: Donald H. Graves, "Child Responsibility in the Classroom." From *Teachers and Learners: A Collection of Narratives from the Second Year of the Mast Way Reading/Writing Research Project*, pp. 158–60. Compiled by Ruth Hubbard and Dori Stratton. Durham, NH: Writing Process Lab, University of New Hampshire, 1985. Reprinted by permission.

10. Host or hostess for any visitors who come to the room. Weekly.

11. Lunch boxes: When children go out to recess at lunch time I have just one or two children bring lunch boxes back to the room instead of having a hoard of children come back. Weekly.

12. Sharing work: A child lines up small and large group sharing for the class. Weekly.

13. Teacher's Personal Helper: Working in the room for the teacher to go get something, put something away, etc. Weekly.

14. Line leader: Get line quiet, lined up, so that it can go down the hall well. Weekly.

15. Kindergarten reminders: Emily handles this, just one child to handle all the complicated schedules for children who tutor kindergarten children. This job doesn't change. There are very few who could probably handle this one.

16. Science Fair: Each group was responsible for the care of its animals: ducks, fish, turtles, frogs, newts, etc.

17. Bulletin boards: The children do up all the letters and materials for the bulletin boards.

Other duties the children handle on their own:

1. Library: The children know that only three can go to the library at any one time throughout the day and that they can't go before 8:45 A.M.

2. New Children: Any new child who comes into the room is the responsibility of one particular child to integrate into the room. We have a new youngster coming tomorrow (May 3rd). Jeff went this afternoon to the office to get two new folders (reading and writing), pencils, and a box of crayons. I picked Jeff because he has the temperament to sustain a whole day with a new child. In a way I don't have that much to do with the child on the first day, as the children here, in particular Jeff, have the responsibility of making the new child feel at home. I suppose if the child went home and the parent asked, "How did you like your new teacher?" the poor kid wouldn't know what to say. In the past, the new children's helpers were:

   Jon—Jessie
   Eddie—Josh
   Laura—Jaime

3. Class speakers: The children handle all contacts with outside speakers for the class. Andy handled this; he was able to contact two different people to come to the room. He did a fine job. Alexia (last year) handled the arrangements with third-grade teacher Ellen Blanchard.

4. Sharing in other rooms: Allan handles this. The children make the contact, then they need to contact Allan to put them on a list. This helps me to see who is coming and going. Allan also reminds the children to keep their appointment in the room where they are sharing.

"Because the children know that they handle most of the major jobs and responsibilities in the room, there are many other things they just plain handle on their own because they know I'd want them to," Leslie told me. "For instance, at share time, they know who is up, and they say, 'OK, Taylor, you can go now.' I just sit there and watch."

From The Meaning Makers

Gordon Wells

The first and most obvious cause of the impoverished interaction that so often occurs between teachers and pupils is the number of children involved—30 or more in the average class, with only a single adult. All of these children have to be kept profitably occupied on tasks that stimulate their interest and promote their learning. The demands on teachers in terms of management, safety, and control are therefore enormous, so it is not surprising to find that there is little sustained interaction.[1] Added to this, at the outset, is the inexperience of children entering school for the first time. They have to learn to behave according to the norms of the classroom, wait while others take their conversational turns, and discuss the shared topic rather than changing the subject at will. The classroom thus suffers from organizational problems that can militate against children's spontaneity and restrict the opportunities for sustained adult-child interaction of the kind experienced in many homes. As a result, the more intellectually stimulating uses of language get submerged under the demands of the sheer number of children to be attended to and the tasks that have to be done in each day.

A second contributory factor seems, more and more, to be the curriculum itself—or, rather, the increasing emphasis on standardization in the interests of accountability with respect to the mastery of the "basic skills." Clearly, it is highly desirable that every pupil should become both literate and numerate and be conversant with certain facts about his or her social and physical environment. But these skills are only of value when they are integrated with the purposes and interests that the pupil brings from outside the classroom. As Barnes puts it, to be useful, school knowledge must be converted into action knowledge.[2]

Too often, though, the concern with the curriculum takes little account of what individual pupils bring to the tasks that they are required to engage in. Instead, curriculum planners concentrate on breaking down what has to be learned into smaller and smaller, relatively self-contained steps, so that they can be arranged into linear sequences for the purposes of instruction. This has led to an exaggerated belief in the efficacy of finely graded, structured programs of work. The problem with this approach, however, is that, while certain types of learning *can* be promoted in this way, it is certainly not the case that children only learn—or even learn most effectively—when all the tasks in which they engage are imposed on them by others in the interests of ensuring a uniform progression through a predetermined sequence. Furthermore, it takes little account of the fact that learning takes place in individual children, each of whom has different interests and abilities; and that, in any class, children proceed at different rates, learning quickly and effectively when they are personally motivated and emotionally stable but more

SCHOOLS AS ENVIRONMENTS FOR LEARNING

Source: From Gordon Wells, *The Meaning Makers: Children Learning Language and Using Language to Learn*, pp. 116–124, 228–29. Portsmouth, NH: Heinemann Educational Books, 1986. Reprinted by permission.

slowly and with greater difficulty when the task seems irrelevant or their personal motivation is low. This is not in any way to suggest that children should not be encouraged to engage in tasks that stretch them, that demand effort and application. But it is to suggest that the commitment that such tasks demand is only likely to be forthcoming if children perceive these tasks to be meaningful and relevant to them.

A further disadvantage of centrally controlled curriculum planning is that the curriculum becomes fragmented into isolated bodies of subject matter, and children are discouraged from making connections between the various topics and types of learning in which they are engaged. In addition, under the pressures that are induced by the perceived need to "cover the curriculum" that is imposed from above, teachers are likely to adopt a didactic style of teaching in which the roles of teacher and pupil are sharply differentiated, with the result that opportunities are seriously reduced for the sort of open-ended, exploratory interaction that encourages children to take some share in the responsibility for planning and pursuing their own learning.

But perhaps the most serious impediment to a more collaborative relationship between teacher and pupil is the mechanistic model of education that is implicit in so much of the discussion about accountability. To talk of the curriculum, or of individual units of work, in terms of "input" and "output" is not only inappropriate in its implicit assimilation of education to the organizational principles and ethics of industrial mass production,[3] but it is also misguided in its simple assumption that well-prepared "input" is all that is needed to guarantee effective learning.

It is not simply that, as has already been stressed, children bring different aptitudes and experiences to each learning task—important though it is to recognize this diversity—but that the learning itself involves an *active reconstruction* of the knowledge or skill that is presented, on the basis of the learner's existing internal model of the world. The process is therefore essentially *interactional* in nature, both within the learner and between the learner and the teacher, and calls for the *negotiation* of meaning, not its unidirectional transmission.

To recognize this essential characteristic of learning is to see in a new light the significance of that well-known precept "Start where the child is." All too often this is interpreted in practice to mean "Administer a test or some other form of assessment in order to decide which ability group to place the child in or which reading primer or worksheet to give him or her." But this is not discovering where the child is—what his or her mental model of the world is like or what his or her current needs and interests are. Instead, it is discovering into which of the places that are prepared in advance the child can most easily be slotted. Really to discover where a child is and, hence, how we can most helpfully contribute to his or her further learning, it is necessary to listen to what he or she has to say—to try to understand the world as he or she sees it. Only then can the teacher's contribution have that quality of contingent responsiveness that we have seen from the preschool years to be essential in helping the child to develop his or her understanding.

The pressure of numbers, the constraints of accountability, and the prevailing mechanistic model of education, then, all tend to reduce the opportunities for a collaborative style of teaching. But perhaps the most insidious influence of all is our own previous experience. Most of us have had many years of being talked *at*, first as pupils and students and, later, during our professional education, both pre-service and in-service. As a result, we have probably unconsciously absorbed the belief that a teacher is only doing his or her job properly when he or she is talking—telling, commanding, questioning, or evaluating. And, in many cases, that is what we see when we look to our colleagues for a model of successful teaching. Despite the lip service that is paid to the "student-centered" conception of education, actual practice tends on the whole to be "teacher-centered," based on a predetermined curriculum at every level from kindergarten to university. It is not surprising, therefore, if, under pressure, teachers tend to fall back on the traditional transmission model of education without realizing how poorly it enables them to fulfill their best intentions.

How, then, can this situation be changed? How can teachers bring their practice more closely into line with the theories to which they probably already subscribe?

There is no simple panacea, of course. But there are a number of changes—some of which every teacher is in a position to make—that are likely to lead towards the style of teaching that has here been described as collaborative.

For many teachers, the first question is, quite naturally: "Will it work?" Of course, the only convincing answer is that of experience—and personal experience, at that. However, there is already the testimony of individual teachers, teaching in many different school systems in countries all over the world. They all say that, having taken the plunge and tried the collaborative style, they would never want to return to their old ways of doing things.

TOWARDS A COLLABORATIVE STYLE OF LEARNING AND TEACHING

But for those who are still undecided, hesitating because of the risks that they perceive to be involved, there is a simple step that will probably be sufficient to convince them that some sort of change is necessary: they could record themselves at work. Before making the recording, they should set down in writing what they hope will be achieved, in particular what types of learning the children will engage in and how their own behavior will contribute. Then, afterwards, they should listen to the tape, noting how far these aims were achieved and, where they were not, asking what were the probable reasons. More specific questions that one might ask are: What are the most frequently occurring patterns of teacher-pupil exchange? Who initiates the interaction, and in which contexts? What sorts of questions are asked, by whom, and for what purpose? Most teachers who undertake this form of self-assessment find that they talk too much, repeat themselves unnecessarily, and give children too little time to respond; they also ask too many questions that restrict children's participation to providing minimal answers requiring only the lowest level of intellectual activity.

If, after making and listening critically to such a recording, it seems desirable to attempt to change, then there are a number of aspects of the total classroom situation that are worth thinking about. First, there is the interactive style itself. Most teachers find that they vary their strategies from one context to another, so it is worth trying to identify those contexts which allow them most readily to engage in genuine collaborative interaction. These can then be developed and the same strategies extended to other contexts. A general principle that almost all teachers find to be rewarding—although initially extremely difficult—is to talk less and to listen more, in particular allowing pupils a longer time to think out what they want to say and giving them time to say it without interruption. It may also be worth thinking about the sorts of questions the teacher asks and about ways of encouraging pupils to ask more questions themselves.

But to focus on language alone may be self-defeating, in the same way that a millipede would probably not be helped by being advised to think about how it was moving one of its legs. More important is for teachers to think about where they are going and which route is likely to be most satisfactory. That means reconsidering what it means to be a teacher in the light of what is known about how children learn and about how others, both adults and other children, can facilitate that learning.

From observations outside school, we know that children are innately predisposed to make sense of their experience, to pose problems for themselves, and actively to search for and achieve solutions. There is every reason to believe, therefore, that, given the opportunity, they will continue to bring these characteristics to bear inside the school as well, provided that the tasks that they engage in are ones that they have been able to make their own. All of us—adults and children alike—function most effectively when we are working on a task or problem to which we have a personal commitment, either because the goal is one that we are determined to achieve (balancing the family budget, repairing a machine) or because the activity is one that we find intrinsically satisfying (writing a poem, building a model), or both. In these circumstances, as the extracts concerning Colin and his model camera show, discussion with someone more skilled or knowledgeable takes on real purpose and significance, as progress to date is reviewed and alternative plans for further work are considered in terms of their feasibility and appropriateness. This is perhaps the teacher's most vital contribution: as a master providing guidance to an apprentice, who utilizes that guidance in the pursuit of his or her chosen goal, the value of which is appreciated by both of them.

For children to achieve this active involvement in their own learning, it is important to find ways of enabling them to share in the responsibility for deciding what tasks to undertake and how to set about them. This does not mean that the teacher should abnegate responsibility or tolerate a free-for-all in which children do exactly as they choose when they choose. Few children can work productively without the support of an understood framework and clear ideas about what is expected of them, and most teachers would not feel that they were adequately fulfilling their responsibilities if they did not provide both guidelines and a clear sense of direction. What is required, therefore, is some form of negotiation in which both pupils' and teachers' suggestions are given serious consideration.

Colin's teacher had devised what were called "choice books," in which the agenda of tasks to be completed was negotiated between the teacher and each individual pupil once each week. At the beginning of the school year, when the children were new to the class, the agenda consisted largely of activities suggested by the teacher. But, as the year progressed, the children began to add their own suggestions and, perhaps more important, to note when they had not yet completed a task satisfactorily or where they needed to make another attempt or gain further information or skill. [The accompanying figure] shows a page from such a choice book.

However, not all teachers will feel comfortable with so much of the curriculum open for negotiation—at least, not initially. It is important to emphasize, therefore, that there is no one correct way to proceed. Indeed, different methods will probably work best for different teachers or for the same teachers with different classes of children. What is important is that, for at least a substantial part of the curriculum, there be genuine negotiation that enables pupils to feel that they have initiated some of their activities and have taken on others and made them their own. "Ownership" is the word that Donald

A Page from a Child's Choice Book

```
January 15th                    Toni
1) Weaving
2) Woodwork. Could you make a loom
   exactly the same size as ours?
3) Study stories. Please use the books
   to learn about the different types
   of stone.
4) Perhaps you and Mandy would like
   to make a book about our plants
   and seeds.
```
```
1) Work at improving your timing game
2) Clay. The books show you different
   ways to make a cup.
3) Work at your sand village.
4) Story writing.
```
```
Wednesday January 17th
To-day I done a Sand village
with mandy and I made a
cup and my hand all came of
and I done a Story and Weaving.
it was good. and my Story is
going to be long and we
tried to make a loom but
it fell a prat
```
```
        Can I do
clay I want to make a
ashtray and a vase.
For my mum.
and the Sand village
and a dolls house.
```
```
January 22nd.
1) Try your loom again but with
   stronger wood.
2) Improve your timing game.
   Ask Kim about hers, it may
   give you some ideas.
3) Create your sand village or could
   you make a model of the school?
4) Begin to make a diary about
   things you have been doing.
```
```
1) Work on your story, so far I think
   it's promising. Please talk to me
   about it again.
2) Work with clay on Monday afternoon.
   I particularly want you to do your
   story today.
   Would you make our model display
   shelves beautiful.
3) Work on your house collage.
4) Shop.
```

Source: Reproduced from *Extending Literacy* (London: Centre for Language in Primary Education, Inner London Education Authority, 1980), p. 25.

Graves uses to make the same point about children's writing,[4] and it applies equally to other activities, right across the curriculum.

When children have a feeling of ownership and share the responsibility for the tasks that they engage in, teachers find that their relationships with the children change. Given responsibility, children behave responsibly and no longer have to be closely supervised every moment of the day. With an agreed agenda, they know what has to be achieved and spend their time productively, using resources appropriately, asking for the teacher's assistance only when other sources have proved inadequate, and moving on to a new task when the present one is completed. As a result, freed from the demands of managing resources, answering trivial questions about procedure, and continually monitoring classroom behavior, teachers are able to spend considerable periods of time with individual children, giving assistance when it is really needed and helping them to reflect on what they are doing and to see how to extend it in various directions.

This, then, is the goal, and these are some of the benefits that are likely to result. But how can it be achieved? Here again, there is no one formula for success, but classroom management—how time, space and other resources are allocated—is one important ingredient. Having the classroom divided into different areas appropriately organized for different activities is an essential preliminary, as is arranging resources—paper, glue, scissors, apparatus, reference books, etc.—so that children can gain access to them without disturbing each other or the teacher. Equally important is the organization of time. Children should have long periods of time to work on the same task, with as few interruptions as possible; and, as has already been implied, they should not all be expected to engage in the same activity at the same time. With individual agendas, there is little danger of this happening, but it will be necessary to ensure an equitable rotation of access to popular work areas and to scarce resources.

These are some of the organizational prerequisites. But perhaps the most difficult question is how to get started. From talking to teachers who have successfully changed their method of working, it is clear that there are many different starting points, ranging from encouraging individual children to pursue a topic that has particularly interested them to proposing a very general theme that individual children are invited to explore in a variety of different ways. Some teachers have made such a theme the center of all curricular activity over a period of one or two weeks; others have developed a theme in the area of social or environmental studies while maintaining their normal pattern of work in the rest of the curriculum. Some teachers have used a work of literature—a story, song, or poem—as the starting point for a wide range of individual activities; one first-grade teacher used the book *Watership Down* in this way, and a teacher of 10-year-olds started with the Prologue to Chaucer's *Canterbury Tales.*

The advantage of a broad theme within which all—or a majority—of the children choose topics to pursue is that there is an overall coherence to the variety of their activities. This is reassuring to the teacher, as it reduces the feeling of being pulled in too many different directions at once. It also has advantages for the children, in that they can more readily work together in groups, collaborating with each other and learning from each other's efforts. Whole-class activities, too, such as visits, reading stories related to the theme, and—most important of all—sharing what each individual or group has created or discovered, have more significance when the theme is one in which all are equally involved.

To teach in this way—collaborating in the pupils' learning and negotiating the curriculum with them—is not easy, of course. It requires a considerable degree of flexibility and an ability and readiness to meet the demands for resources of information and materials that are called for by the interests that the children wish to pursue. It also demands a constant state of open receptiveness to children's ideas and a willingness to take them seriously, even when, from an adult point of view, they seem naive or immature. At the same time, it requires clear thinking and planning in relation to broad, long-term goals and imagination in finding specific themes, activities, and materials that will spark fresh interests and make connections between those that have already been developed.

Some teachers may feel that they are simply unable to meet such demands: that the breadth of their general knowledge is insufficient or that they lack some of the necessary skills. Such doubts are understandable and very real, but they are probably also unnecessary. To teach collaboratively, it is not necessary to know all the answers to pupils' questions or to be already competent in all the skills that an open curriculum may call for. Indeed, a teacher who is universally knowledgeable and competent may actually make it more difficult for pupils to gain confidence in their ability to learn on their own.

Learning is first and foremost a *process*—a continuous making and remaking of meanings in the lifelong enterprise of constructing a progressively more and more effective mental model of the world in which one lives. Learning is never complete.Furthermore, since this process is essentially interactive, it is more helpful for the apprentice learner to work with teachers who are themselves still actively engaged in learning and willing to engage with their pupils in doing so than it is to be instructed and evaluated by those who apparently no longer have the need to engage in such processes themselves.

It is important to emphasize, therefore, that there is no one correct way to proceed. The only really satisfactory solution is the one that each teacher works out for him- or herself, taking into account the particular children concerned, their parents, the school, and its resources and environment.[5]

NOTES

1. In the study carried out by David Wood and colleagues . . . , it was found that as much as 44% of teacher talk was concerned with management (Wood, McMahon, and Cranstoun, *Working with the Under Fives*); and in another piece of research involving 7- to 9-year-olds, the length of most interactions with an individual pupil was 30 seconds or less—barely time for more than a summary evaluation of work carried out or for brief instructions on what to do next. Of course, there were longer episodes, but these were balanced by many more that were much shorter. (Vera Southgate, Helen Arnold, and Sandra Johnson, *Extending Beginning Reading* [London: Heinemann Educational Books, 1981]).

2. Douglas Barnes, *From Communication to Curriculum* (Harmondsworth, Middlesex: Penguin, 1976).

3. I recently heard two educators talking about "tooling up the curriculum" for the following year. Presumably the school was the factory in which the new precision-engineered curriculum was to be installed, with teachers the skilled work-force to operate it and the children the raw material to be processed into acceptably educated members of society.

4. Donald Graves, *Writing: Teachers and Children at Work* (Portsmouth, NH: Heinemann Educational Books, 1982).

5. Most of the ideas presented in this chapter are not new. They can be found in the writings of many of the major educational thinkers of this and previous centuries and in the practice of teachers in the present and the past. Particularly important in the development of my own thinking has been the work of John Dewey who, more than 80 years ago, was putting these ideas into practice in his experimental school at the University of Chicago. His books still have relevance today, particularly *The Child and the Curriculum* and *The School and Society*, published in one volume (Chicago: University of Chicago Press, 1956).

Bibliography

Blackburn, Ellen. "Common Ground: Developing Relationships Between Reading and Writing." *Language Arts* 61 (April 1984): 367–75.

Graves, Donald, and Hansen, Jane. "The Author's Chair." *Language Arts* 60 (February 1983): 176–83.

Harste, Jerome; Woodward, Virginia; and Burke, Carolyn. "Examining Instructional Assumptions: The Child as Informant." *Theory into Practice* 19 (1980): 170–78.

Murray, Peggy, and Hubbard, Ruth. "Classroom Contexts for Language Development, or How to Help Fish Outgrow Their Tanks." Available through The Writing Process Lab, University of New Hampshire, Durham, New Hampshire, 1986.

Hubbard, Ruth. "Structure for Freedom." *The Reading Teacher* (in press).

Writing Conference Principles:
The Child Learns,
The Teacher Learns

Data Sheet for "Writing Conference Principles: The Child Learns, the Teacher Learns"

Note: Zero counter when Heinemann logo disappears.

Segment No.	Beginning	End	Contents
1	00:33	1:41	Pat's introduction
2	1:41	6:15	Pat's conference with Nathan
3	6:15	10:24	Pat's conference with Chris
		CONFERENCE PRINCIPLES	
4	10:24	10:40	Pat's introduction to conference principles
		THE TEACHER FOLLOWS THE CHILD	
5	10:40	11:39	Listening to Nathan
6	11:41	12:08	Active listening
7	12:08	12:44	Interruptions
8	12:44	13:23	Reading back a story
9	13:16	13:34	The child is the expert
		CONFERENCES NEED FOLLOW-UP	
10	13:58	14:16	Follow-up with Chris
11	14:17	14:28	Follow-up with Nathan
12	14:30	15:41	View the writing—and the child—in context
13	15:41	16:22	Pat's conclusion

Suggestions for the Use of "Writing Conference Principles: The Child Learns, The Teacher Learns"

Children are hard at work making meaning out of the barrage of information that surrounds them. Speaking and writing are among the most important tools they can use to help sort through, organize, and form structures for their thinking processes. Speaking and writing are ways to learn.

More teachers are turning to the writing process approach in their classrooms, expecting their children to write and to talk about their writing; but they are uncertain about how to begin to hold conferences with their children. This videotape brings you into the classroom of one teacher, Pat McLure, as she confers with her first-grade students. Pat conducts individual writing conferences with her children between 8:30 and 9:00 every day during writing time. This tape focuses on "real classroom" conference time as Pat talks with the children.

There are many ways to use this tape to help workshop participants become more familiar with writing conference principles. This section presents two ways you might incorporate the tape into workshop situations. These suggestions are meant to be adapted to suit the needs of you and your audience, not followed as a script. But no matter what the situation, it is important for you as the workshop leader to:

- Preview the tape yourself, so that you will be familiar with the contents and can decide how to use it to best meet the needs of your audience.
- Read the accompanying literature in this section of the Resource Guide, as it supplements the information on the tape.
- Provide time for a response to the tape, either by writing or in a discussion.
- Include a time for the workshop participants to plan what their next step will be, based on what they have learned from the information included in the workshop.

FULL-DAY WORKSHOP ON WRITING CONFERENCES

A full-day workshop on writing conferences can be organized and paced as follows:

1. Introduce the writing activity (15 minutes).
2. Choose topics (5 minutes).
3. Provide writing time (10 minutes).
4. Pair off for conferring (10 minutes).
5. Return to large group for discussion (15–20 minutes).

6. Show the tape (20 minutes).
7. Discuss the tape (10 minutes).
8. Read Graves piece (15 minutes).
9. Break for lunch.
10. Distribute transcript and replay portions of the tape (10 minutes).
11. Compile list (15 minutes).
12. Read articles (10 minutes).
13. Brainstorm in groups of three (15 minutes).
14. Return to large group for discussion (20 minutes).
15. Conclude workshop (10 minutes).

One of the best ways to begin a workshop on writing is to have the participants themselves write about topics they have chosen. Then, they can identify with the student's difficulties and successes in the process of composing.

You, as the workshop leader, can begin by thinking of three or four topics—personal experiences of your own. These topics should be of interest to you and should be something you know about.

Tell the workshop participants you will be writing down some topics that you might write about with them. Write down a couple of them, explaining a little about each and why you might write about them. As you are writing your topics, encourage others to number their papers from one to four and list topics from their own personal experiences as well. Three-by-five-inch index cards work well for this exercise. See the example below:

1. Buying Shaker furniture
2. Visiting mother in nursing home
3. Canoe trip
4. Hair cut disaster

After talking briefly about these titles or topics, asterisk or underline one. Instruct the participants to take a few minutes and decide on one of their topics that they could write on for about ten minutes and that they would be willing to share with someone. Encourage them to talk it over with a neighbor if they like.

In about five minutes, begin to write yourself and instruct the other participants to write as well.

After ten minutes, ask your audience to break into groups of two to confer with each other about their writing. The format for these conferences should be as follows:

- The first person reads his or her piece to the partner.
- The partner listens carefully to the piece and, when the reading is completed, responds by telling back what he or she learned from it.

- Then the second person reads his or her piece, and the first person responds by telling back what he or she learned from it.

Allow 10 minutes for this exercise.

After 10 minutes, call the group back together and ask for comments about how it worked. After discussion of a few minutes' duration, ask for volunteers to read their drafts to the whole group, taking responses from the group as they did with their partners.

Now, introduce the tape: "This tape was made from footage gathered in Pat McLure's first-grade classroom during the second year of the Mast Way Research project, conducted by Jane Hansen and Donald Graves. Pat takes us into her classroom as she talks with the children about their writing. Then, she tells us about some of the conference principles that work for her."

Then, show the tape. (This will take about 20 minutes.)

After the tape has finished, ask the workshop participants to respond by discussing what they learned from the tape. In other words, they are responding to it as they would to a piece of writing in a conference. (Allow 10 minutes for this.)

Close for the morning by passing out Donald Graves's "Answers to the Toughest Questions Teachers Ask About Conferences" (pp. 94–99). This piece should help to answer some of the questions that may have arisen in the participants' minds during the course of the morning. Allow 15 minutes for everyone to read the article.

All of this would be a full morning's work, and this point would be a good place to break for lunch.

The afternoon session focuses on what the children know. Begin by passing out the tape transcript (pp. 82–86) as a supplement to replaying the first part of the conference tape (sections 2 and 3, Pat's conferences with Nathan and Chris). Instruct your audience: "As you watch and listen this time, make a note of every time children in the class make a decision on their own. It could be Nathan or Chris, or it could be other children in the classroom."

Then, play back the appropriate sections of tape. (This will take around 6 minutes.)

After playing back those sections of the tape, compile a composite list of all the choices that were made by the children during that section of the tape. It's helpful to make this list on an easel, blackboard, or overhead. (Allow around 15 minutes for this.)

Next, pass out the two pieces "What They Know" and "Spelling" (pp. 100–101 and 106). These narratives were written by adults who worked in Pat McLure's classroom: researcher Ruth Hubbard and Pat McLure herself. Both were coming up with ways to build on what the children know. Take about 10 minutes to read these two pieces, then divide the group into threes to brainstorm some ways that they can build in a similar way on what the children in their classrooms know. (Allow around 15 minutes for this activity.)

Come back into a large group again and spend around 20 minutes discussing both what was learned on the tape and what has been brainstormed for future plans.

Close the workshop by reading aloud "Something Afoul," a short narrative by Tom Romano, a researcher on the Mast Way project who worked in the third grade. (See pp. 102–3). This piece serves as a reminder of the importance of giving children control of their writing.

A shorter workshop on writing conferences can be organized and paced as follows:

1. Introduce the workshop (5–10 minutes).
2. Read article (15 minutes).
3. Show tape (20 minutes).
4. Do a quick-write (10 minutes).
5. Share the writing (10–15 minutes).
6. Take a five-minute break. (This is optional.)
7. Work in groups of three (15–20 minutes).
8. Return to large group for discussion (25–30 minutes).
9. Plan with partner (15 minutes).
10. Conclude workshop (5 minutes).

Begin the workshop by sharing the following quote from Donald Graves (1983), in answer to the question "What's so important about writing conferences?":

> Children discover both new information and the personal satisfaction that goes with knowing something, when they hear the information from their own mouths. And best of all, there is an audience present to mirror the child's knowing.

After sharing the above quote, read aloud "Silent Partners," a short narrative written by Lorri Neilsen, a researcher on the Mast Way project. (See pp. 104–5). This should take around 5 minutes.

Then, in order to give some background information, pass out copies of "Let the Children Teach Us" by Donald Graves (pp. 87–93). Allow about 15 minutes for everyone to read this piece, and when you are sure everyone in the audience has finished, introduce the tape: "This tape was made from footage gathered in Pat McLure's first-grade classroom during the second year of the Mast Way Research project, conducted by Jane Hansen and Donald Graves. Pat takes us into her classroom as she talks with the children about their writing. Then she tells us about some conference principles that work for her."

Then, show the tape. (This will take around 20 minutes.)

When the tape has finished, instruct the workshop audience to do a 10-minute "quick-write"—that is, ask them to take around 10 minutes to write down—in first-draft fashion—what they learned from the tape.

After 10 minutes, ask for three or four volunteers to share their reactions, either by reading what they just wrote or explaining it. Allow around 10–15 minutes for this sharing.

If you are planning a short break, this would be a good time for it.

Then, introduce the next activity: "Pat highlights the importance of following the child and what he or she knows. Let's take a closer look at what Nathan and Chris *do* know, and how Pat is able to respond to their knowledge."

Pass out the transcript of the conferences between Pat and the children (pp. 82–86) and the Response Sheet (p. 81). Now, divide the audience in half, and tell them they will be working in groups of three. Instruct the groups as follows: "Look carefully at the transcript of the conferences between Pat and Nathan and Pat and Chris. Half of you will be working with the first conference, and the rest with the second. On the response sheet, jot down what the child knows, and how Pat responds to that. For example, on the first page of the transcript, Nathan knows that his father saved the fish. Pat responds by repeating back the information in the form of a question, which in turn elicits more information from Nathan. We'll take about 15 minutes to go through these transcripts."

When this activity is completed, call everyone back into one group to share what was learned about the nature of Pat's responses to the children's knowledge. Look for similarities and differences in the two conferences as Pat responds to two very different children and subjects. Allow around 25–30 minutes for the discussion.

After this large-group discussion, ask the workshop participants to choose a partner to work with for the next few minutes. Instructions: "We're going to take a few minutes to help each other make some plans about what your next step will be in using some of the information you have learned today to conduct better writing conferences, or perhaps to begin to have writing conferences in your classroom. One suggestion might be to plan to tape yourself as you confer with a child, and then analyze the tape to see if you followed the child's lead. What did you think you did well? What would you do differently? During the next few minutes, you need to both make some concrete plans and set up a time to get back in touch with your partner for feedback on how it worked out."

After providing about 15 minutes for this planning, call the group back together and close by reading Tom Romano's piece "Something Afoul" (pp. 102–3).

Response Sheet

What the Child Knows	Pat's Response

Transcript of Tape:
Pat's Conferences with Nathan and Chris

PAT'S CONFERENCE WITH NATHAN

Pat: Don't you remember which fish you were writing about?

Nathan: Um . . . oh! *(Reads)* "My swordtail jumped out of my fish tank last week."

Pat: Ohhhh.

Nathan (reading): "My Dad saved it."

Pat: He was able to save it? Get it back in?

Nathan: Yeah, he dunked . . . right . . .

Pat: Dunked it right back in? How are you going to keep it from doing that again?

Nathan: We got a cover.

Pat: Oh . . . *(pause)* So he can't jump out again?

Nathan: No.

Pat: No.

Nathan: My Siamese fighting fish—he can't see the cover—he tries to go up . . .

Pat: Does he?

Nathan: Last night he bumped his nose.

Pat (laughs): He bumped his nose on the cover?

Nathan: Right.

(Kim approaches Pat with her newly published book.)

Pat: Oh, it looks nice, Kimberly. Mm. It is nice, isn't it? Yeah.

Kim: I want to read it to Kristen.

Pat: OK, that's a good idea. *(To Nathan)* So, what else do you have about your aquarium? That's interesting. I like that.

Nathan: That's where I tried to spell "aquarium," but I kind of got mixed up.

Pat: Oh . . . All right. Mmm-hmm.

Nathan (reads): "I got . . . here, I have aquarium. It has lots of fish. I got . . ." *(pause)* I forgot the *a* in there.

Pat: Oh. Right in here?

Nathan: Yeah.

Pat: Yeah, why don't you squeeze one in, then, if you need one there.

Nathan: A little . . .

Pat: Yeah.

Nathan (reads): "I got a Siamese fighting fish. My Siamese fighting . . . fish is a sleepy head today."

Pat (laughs): Mm-hmm. I remember when you wrote that page.

Nathan: Yeah.

Pat: Ok, what else are you going to tell about today? You've told about your swordtail and your Siamese fighting fish . . .

Nathan (reads): "My cat watched my aquarium."

Pat: Oooh. *(pause)*

Nathan (reads): "We . . ."

Pat: Mmm-hmm. *(pause)*

Nathan (reads): "holded him up."

Pat: Oh, so you have to hold him up so he can watch the fish?

Nathan: Yeah, because . . . can't get up on the couch.

Pat: Mmm-hmm. Think he'd like to get some of those fish?

Nathan: Yeah. Once he sees them, his eyes go . . . woomp!

Pat (laughs): Do they?

Nathan: Woomp. 'Cause he thinks . . . *(unintelligible)* . . . the fish.

Pat: He'd like that, uh-huh . . .

Nathan: Yeah, We have to have the aquarium . . . It's my aquarium, anyways, in the living room because it isn't warm enough in my bedroom.

Pat: Mmm-hmm. Mmm-hmm. OK. What else do you have written about your aquarium?

Nathan (turning back to book): This . . . and this . . .

Pat: OK . . . Nathan, you've got a lot of writing.

Nathan (laughs, then reads): "My fish tank is big."

Pat: Mm-hmm.

Nathan: It is, sort of.

Pat: Mmm-hmm.

Nathan (reads): "My Siamese fighting fish did not eat this morning."

Pat: Oh. That was just one day, though, right?

Nathan: Yeah.

Pat: Mmm-hmm.

(Pause)

Nathan (reads): "We got some worms . . ."

Pat: Mmm-hmm . . . Mmm-hmm . . .

Nathan: "To eat" . . . not eat . . .

Pat: I don't know what . . . to

Nathan (reads): "to feed my fish."

Pat (reads): "We got some worms . . ."

Nathan (reads): "On . . ."

Pat: On Saturday?

Nathan (reads): "On Saturday."

Pat: Is that right?

Nathan: Yeah.

Pat: Uh-huh.

Nathan (reads): "To feed my fish."

Pat: Mm-hmm. Did they like them?

Nathan: Yeah.

Pat: Did they? So, now, what else are you going to tell about your aquarium?

Nathan: My snails . . . it's the little snail . . .

Pat: Your snail's getting bigger. Mmm-hmm. Mmm-hmm. Mmm-hmm. So you've still got some more ideas to keep writing about.

Nathan: I think there's a lot of story.

Pat: OK. OK. You've put a lot of information in your book. It's very close to being finished, isn't it?

(Nathan nods.)

Pat: This will be interesting; people will enjoy hearing about it. 'Cause when you've told them about your aquarium, they've had a lot of questions for you, haven't they?

Nathan: I know. Next, I'm gonna write about my skeleton dinosaurs.

Pat: Oh.

Nathan: I have them . . . dimetredon.

Pat: Mmm-hmm. Good. Well, you've got something to write about your snails?

Nathan: Yeah!

Pat: OK.

PAT'S CONFERENCE WITH CHRIS

Pat: How's yours coming, Chris? What'd you do? Oh, is this all about football? Neat!

Chris: That's about Ghostbusters . . .

Pat: Yeah, where does the football story start?

Chris: That . . . that's the football story.

Pat: Oh. Would you read some to me?

Chris (reads): "The Denver Broncos get a break away." I need to take away the . . . the

Pat: Hi, Julie *(a fifth-grade student who comes to Pat's room on Mondays to collect lunch money).*

Julie: Bert needs some . . . change . . . Left over is twenty cents.

Pat: OK. Why don't you just put a note beside it and just say, "He needs change." *(Turning back to Chris)* Did you watch this game?

Chris: No.

Pat: No.

Chris: I made it up.

Pat: This is one you're making up.

Chris: But I'm glad my dad told me.

Pat: Hmmm.

Chris: First, I said, "Maybe Pittsburg isn't a professional team like the Denver Broncos are," and then I asked my dad and he said they were, so . . .

Pat: Mmm-hmm.

Chris: Then I added all these.

Pat: Mmm-hmm. Mmm-hmm.

Chris: That's a little guy. Barry likes that guy.

Pat: So you started putting Pittsburg in your story before you were sure it was the same kind of professional team?

Chris: Um, yeah.

Pat: Yeah? But it worked out fine?

Chris: I kind of, uh, made it up . . .

Pat: Mmm-hmm.

Chris: And I kind of knew it was. But I just wanted to make sure.

Pat: Mmm-hmm.

Chris (reads): "The Denver Broncos got a field goal, but the game is over and the Denver Broncos won."

Pat: So Denver wins, seven to nothing. Pittsburg has nothing. Did you put the goal, the scoreboard on each page?

Chris: Yup. There's the scoreboard.

Pat: Denver seven, Pittsburg nothing. *(Points)* Denver seven, Pittsburg nothing. So it's a Pitts—Denver got the field goal.

Chris: Yeah, touchdown.

Pat: The touchdown, and . . .

Chris: They got the point.

Pat: And then they got the point after, when he kicked the extra point.

Chris: The extra point, yeah.

Pat: Wow! And was it your football helmet that got you started on this?

Chris: Mm.

Pat: Yeah?

Chris: Well, I kinda like the Denver Broncos.

Pat: Mmm-hmm. This is a very good story.

Chris: Anyway, the Denver Broncos lost.

Pat: Did they yesterday? Did they play yesterday?

Chris: Not yesterday. A few weeks ago.

Pat: A few weeks ago? Mmm?

Chris: But they won the Patriots.

Pat: Did they? Did you watch them play?

Chris: The Patriots lost the Cowboys . . .

Pat: Mmm-hmm. That's true. Mm. Are you going to add any more to this football story, or is this one . . . are you going to share this one?

Chris: Yeah, when it's published. I didn't want to share it 'til . . .

Pat: Until after you got it . . .

Chris: 'Cause last time after I shared both my . . . I didn't get to share my published book.

Pat: Oh, how come?

Chris: Because! I already read them a lot of it.

Pat: So, you didn't think they'd be interested in hearing it again?

Chris: Yeah.

Pat: A lot of them have read it to themselves, though. So they must still have an interest in it. 'Cause you've got a lot of names on the card, don't you?

Chris: Um, kinda.

Pat: Yeah.

Chris: Roger got more.

Pat: He's got more names on his card?

Chris: He needs . . . he has a new card.

Pat: So this is the book—this is the story you want to work on next for publishing?

Chris: Yup.

Pat: I think it's a good choice.

Chris: Well, I didn't want to make as much pages because I didn't want to do as many pages.

Pat: Mmm-hmm. But you've told about the game in this book—in this story with this many pages.

Chris: It's only about five pages.

Pat: Mmm-hmm. But if you don't need any more pages to tell the story, you don't need them there.

Chris: Jeff's only has three pages.

Pat: Mmm-hmm. *One* of his.

Chris: It's still a good story.

Pat: Mmm-hmm. Yup. Is that the one he did about Christmas?

Chris: Yeah.

Pat: Yeah? Last year? Mmm-hmm. Yeah, I remember that book. I think that's a good job. We'll be ready to publish it next. Good. Almost picking-up time.

Chris: Maybe this choice time I could choose writing.

Pat: Yup. You can get it typed. Good idea. *(To Roger)* Roger, how's the wasp story coming? . . .

Let the Children Teach Us
Donald H. Graves

Conferences stimulate because they are unpredictable. When children lead conferences, we simply don't know where they will end up. Each conference provides a different journey. Children have different things to teach us, both about their perceptions and interests. We follow and reap the professional benefits of energy given, rather than taken away.

Conferences stimulate children. They stimulate because the child does the work. Children teach, solve problems, answer impossible questions, or discover new information hidden in the recesses of experience. The children can do this when their teachers know it is the child's action that produces the learning.

Teachers let children do the work because the teachers are disciplined. Thomas writes about a new laser weapon that incinerates, and the teacher doesn't try to steer his topic to more humane pursuits. She takes his choice of topic seriously and learns about lasers. Elizabeth searches for a new direction to her paper. The teacher feels the urge to tell her the new direction; she is pressed for time. But she waits and asks questions that help Elizabeth to find her own direction. Janet struggles with spelling; rather than correct Janet's spelling the teacher asks her to underline words she thinks are misspelled. These teachers are disciplined because they take children's intentions seriously, know the writing process, and how children develop as writers.

Conference chapters thus far have shown teachers how to help children to speak and to ask relevant questions. This chapter deals more systematically with the discipline involved when the teacher helps the child to teach and to understand how to develop his own text. When teachers follow in disciplined fashion, conferences can be remarkably different. To show these differences, I include six separate conferences, three each for two children. Just how little the text determines the course of the conference is shown in the outcome, in which teachers follow the children's intentions and perceptions.

Selection I: WEPINS
by Gregory

Ther are mny kds uv wepins ther are had grnad shotrs bazuks flame thrs an mines if you rnt carfull they can kil the gy that has thm if you pull a pen on the grana you hav to thrw it quk or it will blooenup in yr had

Teacher: How is it going Greg?   **CONFERENCE I**

Greg: Good.

Teacher: Tell me about it.

Source: Donald H. Graves, *Writing: Teachers & Children at Work* (Portsmouth, NH: Heinemann Educational Books, 1983), pp. 119–128. Reprinted by permission.

Greg: Well, these weapons will kill you if you don't look out. Some guys forget when they pull the pin and stand there like dopes. It just blows their heads off. What a mess! Other guys get killed too.

Teacher: I see. You do have to watch out for that don't you? And what will you be doing with this piece next?

Greg: Well, they used these to kill Germans and I want to put that in.

Teacher: Fine, go to it.

This conference example lasts forty seconds. Greg is in the midst of writing, is pleased with the information, shares extra information, and has clear plans for what he will write next.

The teacher brings out more information, but Greg has something else in mind for his piece, a section about killing Germans. Greg shouldn't have his writing interrupted any longer, and he is allowed to return quickly to work.

CONFERENCE II

Teacher: How is your piece coming along, Greg?

Greg: Crummy.

Teacher: Well, what isn't going so well?

Greg: None of these words are right. I can't spell and my father'll kill me if this goes home.

Teacher: Are you going to take this home now?

Greg: Nope.

Teacher: Good, then there is time. We'll work on the spelling but not right now. Read the piece to me, Greg.

(Greg is able to read the entire piece without trouble.)

Teacher: Where did you learn so much about weapons?

Greg: All sorts of places, mostly this TV thing they've had on the army in World War II. My grandfather has some weapons from the war cuz he was in it.

Teacher: Greg, I notice that you read your piece without any trouble at all. There is good specific information here. Tell me about your grandfather and those weapons.

Greg: Oh he's got a bayonet, an M-1 rifle. Boy, is that rifle heavy. He said he had to carry it everywhere, and he showed me how to clean it too. My grandfather landed at Salerno in Italy and was badly wounded there. Most everyone got killed around him.

Teacher: I have the feeling you're just getting started on that one, Greg. I mean there's so much more that you know. What are you going to do with the piece now?

Greg: I think I'll just quit right here, but will you help me with the spelling?

Teacher: OK, but first I want you to find seven words that are spelled right (underline those) then circle six that you think you need help with. Do that and then we'll work on it together again.

This conference lasts two and one half minutes. Greg has a self-assessed, nagging problem in spelling. In spite of teacher efforts to divert him to thinking about information, Greg wants help with spelling and won't settle for anything less.

The teacher places the spelling in the "hold" category and asks Greg to read the piece. She wants to know if he can actually read through his spelling and punctuation problems. He can. Her next strategy is to move Greg to teaching her more about the subject. His experiences are rich and detailed, the voice strong. The teacher confidently asks what he will do next with the piece.

The bubble bursts. Greg is still preoccupied with spelling. More writing, in spite of the good information, probably means more spelling which is unacceptable to Greg. He wants help with spelling and finally gets it. First, his teacher needs to know what words he sees as correct and incorrect. They will work on spelling within the framework of his perceptions.

Although Greg has a skills preoccupation, the teacher doesn't want him to lose the perspective of voice and knowing. Ultimately, these will contribute most to the quality of his writing. How easy it would be to cater *exclusively* to the skills. Still, the teacher must deal with his worries and start an approach to help Greg learn to solve his own spelling problems through self-diagnosis.

CONFERENCE III

Teacher: How is your writing coming, Greg?

Greg: Terrific. It's the best.

Teacher: This is one of your good ones?

Greg: Yup, nobody knows more'n me about weapons. My grandfather has lots of weapons.

Teacher: Would you read the piece to me so far?

(Greg reads the piece.)

Teacher: Well, you can read it very well, Greg. And there is a lot about weapons in there, the bazookas, flamethrowers. You've tried to spell some pretty hard words too—grenade, bazooka, blow up. What's the next thing you're going to do with this?

Greg: I'd like to get it published. I think the other kids will be interested in weapons.

Teacher: Do you think this is ready to get published?

Greg: Yup.

Teacher: As it is now, why do you think it is ready to be published? Convince me that it is ready to go as it is.

Greg: Well, I know some of the words aren't right, but I can't spell 'em.

Teacher: I can help with that. There are some important words here that I'd like to see you underline for help. When you want help with a word later for publishing, just underline it. I have another problem, Greg, if I'm going to publish it. I can't tell where some of your information begins and ends. I'd like you to read it aloud again so we can mark it off with some periods and capitals; so I can tell what you want to go together.

(Greg reads his piece aloud with the teacher putting capitals at beginnings and periods where he pauses for meaning units. She then asks Greg to reread, using the markers she has put in, to see if this is the way he wishes the information to sound.)

This third conference is longest (four minutes) because of the extra skills taught at the publishing step. In this conference, Greg has no self-assessed problems. He feels the piece is one of his best and is ready to be published. The teacher seeks to cause intelligent unrest by asking him to convince her that the piece is ready for publishing. The challenge shows that Greg is aware of his spelling problems. Punctuation is another matter.

The publishing step brings more teaching than usual. Greg is asked to underline problem words in spelling; then help is given on marking off meaning units. In this instance, the teacher does the work by putting down the punctuation Greg shows in his oral reading of the piece. She then asks Greg to read his piece, observing the punctuation she has placed in his text. Greg can then see the effect of punctuation markers and decide where the meaning units are best marked.

Selection II: FAR AWAY LANDS
by Mandy

I know a land far away, far away from anything we've seen. I know a special place where a brook runs down a hill, through some daisies, and just as the brook turns to cross the hill another way there is a big, reddish rock. Behind the rock is a moss covered log and in the end of the log is a slight hollow. Place your hand in the hollow and when you feel something soft, squeeze it lightly, feel its coolness, think where you want to be and there you will be. Just like that, faraway from home, troubles, anything you want to leave. So I just go to that place whenever I'm troubled.

CONFERENCE I

Teacher: How is the writing going today, Mandy?

Mandy: I think it's OK, but there is something that isn't quite right.

Teacher: Something is making you itchy?

Mandy: I've been writing for about twenty minutes now, and I like the last part when I get to the hill and the log.

Teacher: Read it aloud to where you are just now.

Mandy: (*Mandy reads the piece aloud*) Well, something isn't quite right there; that's for sure.

Teacher: You said before you liked the last part. How far back does the last part go?

Mandy: (*Rereads again.*) Oh, here it is. Heavens, it goes way back to the first sentence. The first sentence is the funny part. I think I was just putting something down to get started and it's still here. I could start with the second sentence. I'll just line this out.

Teacher: Sometimes lines do stick, make us itchy, and we don't know why. You are early in your draft, and usually it isn't something that should bother you this soon. Later on you'd probably see it more clearly. Still, I guess if it keeps you from going on, you can go back. I do that myself sometimes.

In this example, Mandy is in the midst of composing but is bothered by something in the text. She doesn't feel right about continuing to write. In a short, 2½-minute conference her teacher asks her to reread the piece to sense the problem. Mandy is surprised to find that the first sentence is the intruder. The teacher suggests that writers usually go on, and come back to language questions later, but sometimes, for whatever reason, writers are stymied until they deal with the offensive part.

CONFERENCE II

Teacher: How is your piece coming along Mandy?

Mandy: Great.

Teacher: Where are you in the piece now?

Mandy: Well, I've got it most done. It's about my dreams.

Teacher: Let's take a look. Say, that's quite a scene. I can see where that log is on the hillside. There is good detail—the flowers, the hill, the brook, rock, even into the coolness of the hollow in the log. What are you going to do with it now?

Mandy: I don't know. I sort of figured it was done, that's all.

Teacher: Let's go back to when you decided to write this. What did you have in mind?

Mandy: I've been thinking about this for a long time. I don't really do this. I mean this isn't true. I don't go to a real rock on a hill, and there isn't a log there. But I wish there was. So, I decided to make one here in the writing. I just wanted to make one to see what it was like. That's all.

Teacher: What was it like?

Mandy: Kind of nice, I think. I got the feel I wanted there. Coolness and just a place to go.

Teacher: Yes, that is there. Thank you, Mandy.

Mandy, in this example, is pleased with the piece she has finished. The teacher seeks to find out if the writing matches Mandy's intentions. She first confirms what she sees in Mandy's writing, and then asks the question, "What did you have in mind?" Mandy's answer is precise. She merely wanted to write about the fantasy place she had in mind. She wasn't interested in developing the piece beyond a simple description of the location. Mandy is pleased with the feelings of the place described. The conference ends in less than eighty seconds.

CONFERENCE III

Teacher: How is the piece coming, Mandy?

Mandy: Oh, I'm so confused. I've got started, but I don't know where to go from here. You see, I've got this special place I've created, but now that I've created it, I don't know where to go from there.

Teacher: Turn the paper over for a minute and let's just chat about it. What did you hope to have happen here, Mandy? Where did you want the piece to end up?

Mandy: I wanted to tell about all the things I did when I put my hand in the log. But now I can't think of any. I've just got a big blank; that's all.

Teacher: When you created the log and the cool place, you said you could leave troubles. What kind of troubles?

Mandy: My brother for one. He drives me up the wall. He's a pest. He tattles . . . um, uh, he pulls my hair, steals cookies, and won't leave my stuff alone in *my room*! He's a rat!

Teacher: Well, I can see what you'd leave all right. Now you say you put your hand in the log, touch the cool place . . . Now if you leave your brother behind, what are you going to . . . where do you want to go? I mean, what do you want it to be like?

Mandy: Well, I don't want *him* there. I think it would be pretty quiet. Oh, this is hard. Wait a minute. I'd have a room. That's it. A room the way I wanted it—brother-proof.

Teacher: Sounds as though you know where you are going now, Mandy. You are leaving your brother to go to a room that is starting to take shape. What will you be doing next?

Mandy: That room. I want to think some more about it.

Teacher: The room may take time. No hurry. We can talk about it later if you'd like.

This example shows Mandy in the midst of her draft. She is not sure what to do next with her piece. "You see, I've got this special place I've created, but now that I've created it, I don't know where to go from there." The teacher asks her to turn her paper over in order to discuss the situation. This is a procedure that often helps a writer who has run into a block. The presence of a paper—the half-filled page, the confused line-outs—sometimes needs to be removed from sight in order to discuss the situation afresh. The conference is directed toward Mandy's original intentions. "I wanted to tell about all the things I did when I put my hand in the log."

The teacher tries to broaden the scope of Mandy's thinking by helping her to become reacquainted with some of the ingredients that may have been part of her thinking. "When you created the log and the cool place, you said you could leave troubles. What kind of troubles?" Mandy shares her feelings about her brother. The next question seeks to build a bridge between what Mandy leaves behind and what she might go to as an escape from the past. "Now if you leave your brother behind, what are you going to . . . where do you want to go? I mean what do you want it to be like?" Mandy finds a fresh beginning in thinking about a room. She feels stretched by the question, and has a place to start. The teacher doesn't take the next step for granted and asks, "What will you be doing next?" The conference lasts two minutes.

Conferences with imaginative pieces can be hard work for both teacher and child. Although the piece has a personal narrative base in the escape from her brother, Mandy finds it difficult to create the fantasy, a much more demanding medium for most children. The teacher seeks to aid the imaginative piece by bringing out the personal narrative roots in the writing.

When Discipline in Conference Is Difficult

I am an activist. Each day I make long lists of things I need to do, assigning time allotments for each item on the list. I don't delegate very well. I enjoy the doing so much, I don't want others to have the pleasure of it. I also don't trust others to do the job as well. Their standards wouldn't be up to mine.

If I know something, I can't resist displaying my knowledge. I have a penchant for wanting to inform the world. I have strong ideas about what the world ought to know and the best way to teach it. Certain subjects I think are irrelevant, a waste of time, not worth the doing. *I ask others to deal with my priorities.* My voice is heard in the next room. Other teachers shut their doors when I teach.

How hard it is for an activist to conduct conferences! Everything is reversed. I have to give up the active, nondelegating, pushing, informing role for another kind of activity, the activity of waiting. Action in conferences is redefined as intelligent *reaction*. The child must lead, the teacher intelligently react.

Learning this new discipline has been a conscious pursuit for me in the last seven years. There is hardly a conference where I don't meddle, make some portion of it mine. I simply can't resist leaving my mark, my finger prints, or my initials in the corner of the work. But the rewards, the new energy as the learner teaches me, keep me going. The margin of writer control increases while my presence decreases. Gradually, I've become aware of those times when I don't follow and play the active-controlling role. Here is a list of some of the checks that tell me when I'm back in my old active role:

- I talk more than the writer.
- I try to redirect the writer to a subject that is more interesting to me.
- I try to redirect the writer to a more morally uplifting subject.
- I ignore where the writer is in the draft.
- I ignore the writer's original reason for writing the piece.
- I teach skills too early in conference.
- I supply words, catchy phrases, and examples for the writer to use. (I'm delighted if the writer uses *my* language.)
- I ask questions I *know* the writer can't answer.

Writing demands discipline, the waiting response. The marvelous part about waiting for children, and helping them to teach us, is what we learn ourselves. Seven-year-olds will teach us about space, cats, dogs, prehistoric animals, their ills, and fantasies about wild creatures from outer space. They send us scurrying for reference books when they reverse roles and ask *us* questions. The top teachers, I've found, whether in the center of the city or in a rural school, have an insatiable appetite for learning. When teachers learn, the children learn.

Answers to the Toughest Questions Teachers Ask About Conferences

Donald H. Graves

This chapter is a workshop on the ten most common questions asked about the conduct of conferences. The questions discussed are those that have risen from practitioners who have tried to conduct conferences . . . ; the answers here tend to be oversimplified but give the reader a chance to see a framework within which to deal with similar questions.

Questions have been divided into two categories:

1. Questions ancillary to the conduct of conferences.
2. Questions relating to practices within the conference.

ANCILLARY QUESTIONS

Ancillary questions deal largely with the conference setting:

1. How do I find time to do conferences?
2. How often should I have conferences with each child?
3. What are the other children doing when I have my conferences?
4. What's the easiest way to keep records of conferences?
5. How can I tell if I'm improving in my conduct of conferences?

1. How Do I Find Time to Do Conferences?

Teachers usually ask this question because they view the conference as the replacement for written remarks on children's papers, feeling that every paper needs to be "corrected" and that the conference is the means to do this. The teacher rightfully wonders, "And how am I going to find the time to get to each child to do all that correcting?"

Conferences work because time is used differently by both teacher and child. Children use time differently because as soon as they finish one piece, they start another. They don't wait for teacher "approval" before going on with their writing. The paper goes in a completed work folder for the teacher to read that night. In short, writing is a continuous activity for the child. The usual questions, "What'll I do now, I'm done?" are not relevant in this kind of teaching.

Conferences also work because the teacher has a different time frame for evaluating their effect. Conferences have a cumulative effect on the writer. After four or five conferences with a teacher, writers usually display more initiative because they have found their subjects, can speak about them, and

Source: Donald H. Graves, *Writing: Teachers & Children at Work* (Portsmouth, NH: Heinemann Educational Books, 1983), pp. 141–48. Reprinted by permission.

assume responsibility for their success. For some writers this period may take longer, especially for older children, since dependency withdrawal is much more complicated.

Teachers also use time differently because of the way they structure responses during a writing period. Within a thirty-seven-minute framework the teacher might confer with children according to this sample timetable:

A. *First ten minutes*—children who need immediate help. From folders reviewed the night before the teacher decides on the six or seven children who need immediate response. These may be handled in a "roving" type conference, moving from seat to seat among the children who are writing.

B. *Next fifteen minutes*—children who are regularly scheduled. The number of children in the room are divided by days in the week, and then assigned to a Monday, Tuesday, etc. group. They meet the same day each week to talk about the progress of their writing. They bring their folders and are prepared to discuss their current piece.

C. *Next twelve minutes*—individual conferences. The teacher meets with four or five children who are at important stages in their piece. This may also be a clinic group of five children who are brought together because they are ready to apply a common skill to their papers.

The above plan has the teacher responding to about seventeen children in a normal writing morning.

Realize, if you are a teacher just starting conferences, that first conferences *take longer*. As both you and the children learn what conferences are about, they get both shorter and longer: shorter because the child takes more responsibility; longer because you learn when significant teaching moments arise. Two or three ten-minute conferences every two weeks are justified as the writers learn to take more responsibility.

2. How Often Should I See the Child in Conference?

This varies with the child. Children who struggle with writing, particularly bright children in transition, and those who are alarmed at the discrepancy between their intention and their performance, need to be seen daily, probably for no more than thirty seconds. Every child, as mentioned in answer to the last question, needs to be seen once a week. Later, as writing time moves more smoothly and more children are learning to use it well, a growing number need be seen outside of regular conferences but at least once every two weeks. Again, the *cumulative effect* of conferences makes itself felt in the growing independence of the writers.

3. What Are the Other Children Doing During Conference Time and How Do I Keep Them From Interrupting Me?

The other children are writing. They write continuously. When one piece is finished they start another. The children make a growing list of topics on which to compose. It is the child's responsibility, with some help, to keep his list of topics up to date. This list is usually best kept on the inside cover of his writing folder.

In some classrooms, writing is handled within blocks of time. That is, in a morning period, writing is one of the child's responsibilities along with reading, math, and science. This type of classroom usually has learning centers well stocked with good, self-directed activities.

Children usually interrupt teachers in conferences for three common reasons. First, they don't yet understand the significance of what they are doing. This is particularly true of very young children. Second, procedures for solving problems in the room may not be clear cut. Third, the terror of the blank page, the loneliness of writing, is overwhelming. They seek company . . . yours!

I ask very young children (six through eight) in group meeting to tell me what I am doing in conference. I am interested in their changing impressions of what happens. "If I am working with Margaret, and Sarah should interrupt me, what might happen?" I ask the class. It is not unusual for young children (and some older ones as well) to think that if the teacher is not working with *them*, nothing of significance is going on.

The next area to give attention to in teaching is classroom procedures. Mechanical problems—paper storage, use of lavatories, keeping writing folders, storing completed work, use of writing instruments and art supplies etc.—all need to be worked out with the children. The lack of provision for any of these can lead to a conference interruption. Every class has its own procedures. Handle new conference interruptions in a group session, "Well, how can we solve this one?"

There will always be a certain level of interruption with very young children. The explosive joy of completing a paper just has to be shared. Fifteen seconds of receiving is enough.

More difficult is the child in transition, the child fraught with the restlessness of an idea pecking its way to the surface. Most children are helped by class share sessions on "what to do when you are stuck on. . . ." Discussions center on such problems as what to do if you can't:

- spell a word
- think of the next thing to write in your draft
- figure out the one thing your piece is about
- think of the next topic.

4. What's the Easiest Way to Keep Conference Records?
Keep them simple or they won't be used. At first I keep a notebook with each child's name on a tab for easy reference. The page is already lined off, leaving a little room for writing. The entry (spelled out in more detail in Chapter 28) looks like this:

Oct. 10	A Skunk I Saw
(Date)	(Title)
	+
(Skill)	(Rating)
Good experience and involvement in piece.	
(Note)	

No more than fifteen seconds are required for the entry. At a glance the page reports the title of the piece, content, skills covered, and a rating on the overall quality of the conference. This usually is enough information to help recall further details of the conference. Early on, when we often do more talking than the child, record keeping is particularly difficult. Later, more elaborate record-keeping systems are possible if you need them.

5. How Can I Tell If I'm Improving in My Conduct of Conferences?
This question is not necessarily one that teachers ask directly in a workshop. However, it is often the unasked question underlying all others. Teachers want to be better at what they do. They want to help children become good writers.

The important thing is to keep your perspective on the entire writing program and the conferences within it. Here are some do's and don'ts on maintaining a balanced view of what you are doing:

1. Don't decide the failure or success of a program on the basis of one class. Take an eight-week frame and review progress in all folders.
2. Don't decide conference success on the basis of three or four children who don't seem to handle conferences well. In a class of thirty, there will *always be three to five children* with whom *no teacher* relates as well as hoped. This doesn't mean the teacher dismisses the children as hopeless; the search continues, but it shouldn't affect your total view of what is happening with other children.
3. At the end of eight weeks, look over your conference records to see which children ought to receive more time, which less.

Keep tape-recorded samples of your conferences with children who do well and those with whom you struggle. When you listen to the recording, note:

1. The balance of your talking and the child's.
2. How much did the child teach you about the subject? How much did you learn? How could you have learned more?
3. What responsibilities did you take that could have been given to the child? Were the responsibilities within the child's developmental level?
4. Did the child understand what to do next in the writing?

Video tape recordings open an extra dimension. The same questions are asked of conference content as in audio recording, but video taping allows more self-assessment:

1. How did you physically relate to the child? Does your distance change with different children?
2. How did you and the child hold the work? Who holds the work and why? What does this have to do with who "owns" the writing?
3. Were there any physical barriers (table, room) that stood in the way of a successful conference?

Here are several questions about conference practice:

1. What's the best way to start to use conferences?
2. How do I shorten conferences . . . take less time?

CONFERENCE
PRACTICE
QUESTIONS

3. How do I do less talking . . . the children more?
4. What do I do when the piece has major problems and the child thinks it is good the way it is?
5. How can skills be taught in conference? Seems to me skills should be taught with much larger groups.

1. What Is the Best Way to Start Conferences?

The easiest way to begin conferences is to concentrate on one thing, the child's information. Since the children are not used to coming to more formal conferences at a teacher table, just move around the room, "roving" from child to child. As you look at each paper, receive the information using the child's own words: "I see you know that pterodactyls fly." Follow with a question that extends the information; help the child to teach you: "How did you know that? Pterodactyls look too big to fly. How do they do that?"

2. How Do I Shorten Conferences . . . Take Less Time?

Teach one thing, no more. Make it a discipline to choose one thing to teach, realizing that retention from conferences is high. The tendency when first working with conferences is to overteach, since the teacher feels that it may be a week before she meets with the child again. Overteaching means the child leaves the conference more confused then when he entered.

After several months, conferences can be shorter because both teacher and child know how to function together. Remember to expect children to speak first about three things: "What is the piece about, where are you in the writing, and what help might you need?" When children speak first, much time is saved.

3. How Do I Do Less Talking, the Children More?

Don't feel the pressure of time. Teachers talk more when they feel rushed. Teachers wait better when they realize that even two high-quality conferences a month contribute *significantly* to the growth of a writer. Remember, writers can go a lifetime and not get responses to their writing in draft. When children sense that you are waiting, that they have as long as ten or fifteen seconds (a long time) to respond, to speak about what they know, they talk.

Expect children to talk first. Children will talk first if they find that the information they share is used to help them say more; that the teacher is interested in their subject no matter what the topic. It is hard work to help children know what they know.

4. What Do I Do When the Piece Has Major Problems and the Child Thinks It Is Good the Way It Is?

First, ask the child why he thinks it is good. Take the child at his word. It may be that the child's reasons will change your view of the quality of the piece. The child should be asked to tell the teacher why a piece is good far more often than is the actual practice. If the teacher doesn't ask, the child loses a chance to gain experience in talking about writing, and the teacher loses insight into the child's criteria for deciding what is good.

The child may be delaying a real decision about the quality of his paper. If there are problems of meaning with the piece, I'll choose a section for teaching, one that I believe the *child knows well*, or which demonstrates a skill the *child can handle*. The question I address to the child concerns problems of meaning: "Tom, I can't understand this part here. How did the boys get back on the horse?" I ask about getting back on the horse because it is an important part that is missing. If the problem in a piece is a matter of a skill, the issue of meaning is still in the question. "I can't understand this part. What did you mean? The way you told it, you had two separate ideas. How can these be separated on the paper?"

5. How Can Skills Be Taught in Conference? Why Not Do Them in Group Settings Instead?

Skills are taught in conference because they last longest when they are taught within the context of the child's own paper. Skills lose their usefulness as tools when done as isolated drills on master sheets. Fewer skills are called to the child's attention this way, but those that are become part of the child's practicing repertoire.

Some skills can be taught in a group setting. A teacher reviews folders and finds that six children need to talk about quotation marks because they have characters who are speaking in their papers. A small workshop is conducted where each child finds characters who are speaking in his own paper. Then the child identifies where the speaking begins, and where it ends. The children then look for other places where people have spoken in their papers.

What They Know

Ruth Hubbard

8:30 A.M. Monday morning. As usual, the children in Pat McLure's first grade headed straight for their writing folders. But my agenda was slightly different from usual. Pat and I are wrestling with finding a procedure to record the children's progress—one that will be both easy enough to keep up and a help to the children. So this morning, I decided to consciously look for what the children *can do*, share the information with them, and begin to record that data.

Chris W. was hard at work on his epic tale of the family trip to Maine. When I slid into the seat next to him, he offered to read his piece, carefully explaining the pictures as well.

"See? This is a back view of me over the fence." He picked up his pencil and carefully wrote, "SO I HAD TO GO THO THE FANS."

After a brief discussion of his piece, I pointed to his last sentence. "Chris, I notice you leave spaces between the words in your writing."

Chris nodded. "Yeah, you need to so you can read the words back."

Roger inched closer, glanced at Chris's paper, then his own story.

"Some kids don't leave spaces," Chris went on, "so they have trouble when they want to read it."

Now Jenny looked down at her paper where a row of letters marched across the paper. "I can't read this back, 'cause I wrote it Friday," she confessed.

I showed Chris my notebook. "I'm writing down that you know to leave spaces between words," I told him and the other listeners at the table. "That's a helpful thing to remember."

As I circulated among the other writers, I enjoyed short conferences with several children. Noa talked about a special Hanukkah cup in her drawing, Kristin showed me her new Cabbage Patch eraser and the piece she's started about it, and Roger shared information he's learned from his new spider book.

Tara was chattering gaily as she wrote her piece: IT IS FOD GOING TOBRTDAY PRTE. "It is fun going to birthday parties," she read. In our short conference, I learned that all birthday parties are fun, but especially Adrienne's, because it was held at Chuck E. Cheese.

"Tara, I notice that you know all the letters that make the 'ing' sound," I told her, pointing to the word 'going.'

"Yes, I really do," she agreed. "Not just for 'going,' either. And I can read it, too. I can read, you know. I can read *Goodnight, Moon*."

She jumped up, ran to the book area, and hurried back with a copy of *Goodnight, Moon*. She flipped through the pages, reading some and inventing others. Sure enough, when she came to the words "jumping," "whispering,"

Source: Ruth Hubbard, "What They Know." From *Teachers and Learners: A Collection of Narratives from the Second Year of the Mast Way Reading/Writing Research Project*, pp. 18 –19. Compiled by Ruth Hubbard and Dori Stratton. Durham, NH: Writing Process Lab, University of New Hampshire, 1985. Reprinted by permission.

and "sitting," she read them, always exchanging a special look with me to show me she *knew* she could both read and write that 'ing' sound.

When I shared my morning's harvest of data with Pat, she was pleased, and decided we should slip a sheet of oaktag into the children's folders to record the things the children know how to do for their own use. Later, she wrote to me. "There is such a good positive reinforcement to recording what they are doing correctly—what they know. As you mentioned today, it should rub off on some of the others sitting around the table. Chris W. was using spaces between his words and now there are three more children who know that it's important."

Something Afoul

Tom Romano

[Conferences] are not for making the product better; they are for teaching control of the process, letting the writer gain insights.

And there I was on Tuesday morning, sitting beside pilot Melissa, acting as insistent co-pilot, pushing for product, aching to take over the controls—just for awhile, just enough to throw her into a tailspin. Last week Melissa had written "My Christmas," a seven-page narrative in which she described her anticipation of Christmas, the arrival of her long-distance relatives, and the opening of presents. The first draft was neat, the words carefully printed on every other line.

The week before she had read the story to me and, when I chatted with her about it, had told me some marvelous details. Among them, "I tried to make my mind go blank, but all I saw were Christmas trees." I asked if she would add that. No, she wasn't inclined to. We talked more about the story. Finally, when Jan called all the kids to large-group sharing, I told Melissa, "I wouldn't have known the Christmas trees detail from the story. I'd like to see you add that because it is a one-of-a-kind Melissa detail." She wasn't fazed. She smiled—at my impetuosity, I imagined—and headed off to the share session.

Adult pressure. No thumbscrews, mind you, but definite, applied pressure. I gave her more that Tuesday. I brought in a rough draft of a piece I'd written, showed her its messiness, the cross-outs, the added marginalia. She showed moderate interest, then got out her Christmas story, ready, she said, for revision. She read through the piece, stopping a dozen times to ask her friend Amy and me questions about correctness—mainly spelling and punctuation.

I asked her if she'd read the piece to any of her classmates. She hadn't.

"Are you going to?"

"No."

"How come?"

"Because I want this to be mine, my story. Oh, I don't know!"

The appearance of Melissa's first draft resembled a newly written second or third draft, few additions, few deletions, few corrections. She wanted it neat so the typist could read it. Jessica, across the table, said, "I know my first draft is going to be messy, so I just let it get messy, then I make a new one."

None of that for Melissa. Seven pages is a lot to recopy. This draft was it.

Later, on the playground, I talked to Jan Roberts, Melissa's teacher, about my morning, about my irresistible urge to get Melissa to improve the written product, especially since I saw so much potential in it.

Source: Tom Romano, "Something Afoul." From *Teachers and Learners: A Collection of Narratives from the Second Year of the Mast Way Reading/Writing Research Project*, pp. 92 –93. Compiled by Ruth Hubbard and Dori Stratton. Durham, NH: Writing Process Lab, University of New Hampshire, 1985. Reprinted by permission.

"Well," she said, "you're used to working with older kids. Melissa's just eight. I noticed that the piece had a lot of voice."

That it did.

"Maybe," continued Jan, "this is just going to be her voice piece."

Writer variability. I must keep that in mind. And I must keep in check my ever-present urge to improve every emerging product. If the kids write plenty, there will be ample time to do revision, to practice that critical kind of discovery. I've seen Melissa revise extensively in the past. She'll do it again.

Silent Partners

Lorri Neilsen

David Diller and I sat at the table in Marion's classroom the other morning to have a pre-publishing conference on his story about him, Matt, and two young girls riding off together into the woods on an ATC and a snowmobile. With those big innocent eyes and with that mischief curled around his mouth, David Diller doesn't have to say a word. He is already eloquent. In fact, with such eloquence, David could well be riding off into the forest with fair damsels for a good many years to come.

We huddled over the table. To an observer, it may have seemed that David and I were seldom speaking. But David and I knew otherwise. For David (who has the most articulate eyes I've seen in a while) and me (who believes silence speaks volumes), the next fifteen minutes were non-stop conversation.

David handed me his paper, which was his last draft before publishing, and told me to correct any errors I saw on the page. "I have another idea," I said. "You read your story aloud to me and tell me what you think needs to be changed. We'll talk about it, and then *you* make the changes."

(*Did you hear me emphasize* you, *David? This is not idle chatter here. I'm talking philosophy of teaching. This is* your *piece of writing. It's like your room, your Lego fort. Just because I'm older and bigger doesn't give me the right to come in and mess with your writing. Fight for ownership.*)

David looked at me a long time. Those eyes were sizing me up. Finally, he sighed and shrugged his shoulders. "Okay," he said.

(*Sure, lady; we'll do it your way. I don't know what you're so excited about.*)

We moved our chairs closer and began to pore over the lines. David soon noticed that he interchanged the words "me" and "David" and it didn't sound right. So he turned over his short pencil and began to erase. Each time David wanted to change a word, he would grind the remnants of the eraser into the paper. Sometimes, he repeated his earlier mistake and had to erase twice on the same spot. The paper was becoming grey-brown and wrinkled, the letters barely comprehensible. "David," I suggested, smiling as sweetly as I could, "since you're planning to write this on good white paper straightaway, do you want to try crossing out the words and writing beside them, or using an arrow to point to your correction?"

(*David, watching you repeatedly attack that flimsy piece of newsprint with that dirty, stubby eraser is driving me bananas. Give me that wretched pencil and go get a clean sheet of paper.*)

David looked at me and blinked. "No," he said simply.

(*You want ownership? You got ownership. I started this story on this sheet of paper and I'm going to finish it on this sheet of paper. And it's going to be perfect.*)

We carried on, one step at a time. We had just about reached "snow-mobile" when we heard a voice from behind. "Can I go to the library?" the

Source: Lorri Neilsen, "Silent Partners." From *Teachers and Learners: A Collection of Narratives from the Second Year of the Mast Way Reading/Writing Research Project,* pp. 107–10. Compiled by Ruth Hubbard and Dori Stratton. Durham, NH: Writing Process Lab, University of New Hampshire, 1985. Reprinted by permission.

voice said. David looked at me. I was looking at the paper. The voice grew louder. "Can I go to the library?" The question was obviously directed at me. I looked at David and smiled, pointing at his paper. Those eloquent eyes seemed to hold a question.

(*Lady, are you deaf?*)

I pointed to the word "snowmobile." "Okay," I said to David, "So far, so good. Read this and see how you'd spell it differently."

(*Let's carry on, kid. This is our time. Your time. This person knows we're in conference.*)

Again the voice: "Can I go to the library?" Again, David's eyes.

(*What's going on here? Are you going to answer him or aren't you?*)

Again, I pointed to the word "snowmobile." "You know most of it," I said as he turned back to the page. And he did; he was able to get all but "ile" on his own, and we moved on. We talked about the "two–to's" and about "sleeping bags." He seemed happy about spelling "sleeping bags" right. And at one point, after a quick glance at me to see if I was looking, David abandoned the eraser on a particularly greased-up part of the paper and used arrows instead. He smiled at me.

(*Okay, so I took your suggestion. It's no big deal.*)

We were both into it now. David knew how to change a "two" and in the excitement ripped a big hole into the paper. We both laughed.

Suddenly we heard, "Will you read this for me?" *Process interruptus* was back. This time, David didn't even look at where the voice was coming from. He looked at me.

(*Are we going to go through this again?*)

I pointed to the sentence we were working on. He looked down at the paper. "I know this one," he said, as he made a change. The voice behind David and me grew louder, but we carried on. He didn't hear it anymore. We were finally alone in the busy room.

David smiled as he finished his correction. "Is this the right 'two'?" he said. "It's the right 'two,'" I said.

(*Now this team's warming up, kid. It's your ball.*)

I heard one voice say to another, "They won't answer you," and David and I smiled. We were almost finished with the paper. We had passed "sleeping bags" earlier and now, writing about what he and Matt were planning to do in the tent, David saw he had written "slep." I opened my mouth to say, "You try spell . . ."

You could have heard the synapse down the hall. He put his hand up as if to push me back. "Don't tell me!!! Don't tell me!!!" His grin was bigger than a baseball field.

(*This is my fly ball, lady. I know how to spell "sleep" now.*)

He made the change, held up his paper, and leaned back. We were both grinning like fools. "I'm pretty good, aren't I?" he said. And he leaned forward over his paper, not even waiting for an answer.

Spelling

Pat McLure

If you ask a class of first graders what they know how to spell, be prepared, because they know a lot. The variety of words in their spelling vocabulary far exceeds any spelling list we might assign to them.

In January, I started asking the children in my class to spell a word each day. It could be any word of their choice. We have this spelling lesson each morning sitting in a circle in the classroom meeting area. When I started, I thought of it as a positive way to reinforce the idea that there are conventional spellings for words. Well, it accomplishes that, but a lot more happens as well. Our spelling time has become a time to share experiences, affirm friendships, learn about geography or phonetic patterns, and hear about family members.

In looking back through our master list on which I record everyone's words, I see lots of names. Children have spelled names of people, cities, and countries, book titles, soccer teams, brands of sneakers, and names of pets. It becomes a public announcement of friendship when one child spells the name of a friend and the friend spells his name in return. The children share some news or an experience by spelling a name. Tara had a new cousin born recently, and it took her three days to learn to spell "Jacqueline." Katherine spelled "Epcot Center" after her trip to Florida, and Barry spelled "Ireland" and "Bunratty Castle" after his trip.

Some children have followed word categories. Chris spelled a color word each day, and Noa spelled a number word. Jill got interested in birds and practiced their names at home and at school. She spelled "robin" and "cardinal," "goldfinch" and "bluebird." Then Chris became interested, and she helped him learn some birds' names.

Many times the children's words lead us into a short phonics lesson. It's easy to look through the list and pick out some words with the short *a* sound, or ones with a long vowel and silent *e*. On one day, Nathan spelled "moving," Bobby spelled "missing," and Barry spelled "jumping." That was the day we talked about adding the ending *-ing* to a word.

Long words were popular for a while. "Mississippi" was spelled by several children. Then Adrienne added "xylophone" to her list, Dwayne spelled "kangaroo," Barry spelled "battleship," and Kimberly learned "television."

There seems to be no shortage of ideas. The list will continue to grow until the last day of school in June.

Source: Pat McLure, ''Spelling.'' From *Teachers and Learners: A Collection of Narratives from the Second Year of the Mast Way Reading/Writing Research Project*, pp. 164–65. Compiled by Ruth Hubbard and Dori Stratton. Durham, NH: Writing Process Lab, University of New Hampshire, 1985. Reprinted by permission.

Bibliography

Graves, Donald H. "All Children Can Write." *LD Focus* 1(1) (Fall 1985), 36–43.

Hansen, Jane. "Teacher's Share." *The Reading Teacher*, May 1985, 836–40.

Hansen, Jane, and Graves, Donald H. "Do You Know What Backstrung Means?" *The Reading Teacher*, April 1986.

Hubbard, Ruth. "Write-and-Tell." *Language Arts*, October 1985.